preach it!

Flagship church resources
from Group Publishing

Innovations From Leading Churches

Flagship Church Resources are your shortcut to innovative and effective leadership ideas. You'll find ideas for every area of church leadership, including pastoral ministry, adult ministry, youth ministry, and children's ministry.

Flagship Church Resources are created by the leaders of thriving, dynamic, and trend-setting churches around the country. These nationally recognized teaching churches host regional leadership conferences and are respected by other pastors and church leaders because their approaches to ministry are so effective. These flagship church resources reveal the proven ideas, programs, and principles that these churches have put into practice.

Flagship Church Resources currently available:

- *60 Simple Secrets Every Pastor Should Know*
- *The Perfectly Imperfect Church: Redefining the "Ideal Church"*
- *The Visual Edge: Compelling Video Connectors for Your Worship Experience*
- *Mission-Driven Worship: Helping Your Changing Church Celebrate God*
- *An Unstoppable Force: Daring to Become the Church God Had in Mind*
- *A Follower's Life: 12 Group Studies On What It Means to Walk With Jesus*
- *Keeping Your Head Above Water: Refreshing Insights for Church Leadership*
- *Seeing Beyond Church Walls: Action Plans for Touching Your Community*
- *unLearning Church: Just When You Thought You Had Leadership all Figured Out!*
- *Morph!: The Texture of Leadership for Tomorrow's Church*
- *The Quest for Christ: Discipling Today's Young Adults*
- *LeadingIdeas: To-the-Point Training for Christian Leaders*
- *Igniting Passion in Your Church: Becoming Intimate With Christ*
- *What Really Matters: 30 Devotions for Church Leadership Teams*
- *Discovering Your Church's Future Through Dynamic Dialogue*
- *Simply Strategic Stuff: Help for Leaders Drowning in the Details of Running a Church*
- *Preach It!*

With more to follow!

preach it!

By Stuart Briscoe

Flagship church resources
from Group Publishing

preach it!

Copyright © 2004 Stuart Briscoe

(An updated version of *Fresh Air in the Pulpit* published by Baker Books)

Visit our Web site: www.grouppublishing.com

**Published in association with the literary agency of Alive Communications,
Inc., 7680 Goddard Street, Suite 200, Colorado Springs, CO 80920.**

Credits
Creative Development Editor: Paul Woods
Chief Creative Officer: Joani Schultz
Editor: Candace McMahan
Copy Editor: Linda Marcinkowski
Art Director: Jean Bruns
Book Design & Production: Toolbox Creative
Cover Art Director: Jeff A. Storm
Production Manager: Peggy Naylor

Library of Congress Cataloging-in-Publication Data
Briscoe, D. Stuart.
Preach It! / by Stuart Briscoe.—2nd pbk. ed.
    p.   cm.
    Includes bibliographical references.
    ISBN 0-7644-2644-3 (pbk. : alk. paper)
    1. Preaching. I. Title.
    BV4211.3.B75 2003
    251—dc22   2003016657

10 9 8 7 6 5 4 3 2 1   13 12 11 10 09 08 07 06 05 04

Printed in the United States of America.

Dedicated to the memory of the first preacher I ever heard—my father, Stanley Briscoe (1904–1959)

A *faithful* man

contents

···

Chapter 1: "Preach It, Lad, Preach It!"...........................9

Part 1: Preparing the Preacher
Chapter 2: The Preacher's Power Source 21
Chapter 3: Who Dares to Preach? 31
Chapter 4: Faithfulness Required 41
Chapter 5: Preaching Under Pressure........................ 49
Chapter 6: More Pressure for the Preacher 59
Chapter 7: Dealing With Personal Pressure............... 65
Chapter 8: Putting Things in Perspective................. 71

Part 2: Preparing the People
Chapter 9: "The View From the Pew"....................... 85

Part 3: Preparing the Message
Chapter 10: Developing a Preaching Plan................. 101
Chapter 11: Preparing a Sermon 113
Chapter 12: Pointers on Proclamation 125
Chapter 13: Developing Introductions 135
Chapter 14: Including Explanations and Applications............. 143
Chapter 15: Crafting Conclusions 161

Part 4: Time to Let Yourself Go
Chapter 16: Being a Free and Joyful Preacher 169
Chapter 17: Speaking With Freedom 179
Additional Reading.. 189

chapter ❶

....

"Preach It, Lad, Preach It!"

Fifty-five years ago I preached my first sermon. And nobody was more surprised than I. At the tender age of seventeen, I had recently left high school and embarked upon a career in banking courtesy of the District Bank, a British financial institution that initially paid me a pittance but promised me a good pension forty-eight years hence! So I was, apparently, settled for life like the other men in the branch, many of whom had been keenly anticipating retirement for almost forty years. But God had other plans. Having been transferred far from home by the bank, I attended a small church as a stranger and was startled when a gentleman approached me and asked, "How old are you?"

I replied "Seventeen."

"It's time you were preaching," he pronounced confidently.

To which I replied timidly, "I can't preach."

He inquired, "Have you ever tried?" When I replied in the negative, he responded with relentless logic, "How, then, do you know you can't do it?" I was duly mortified. But it got worse. "You will preach next Tuesday to the youth group, and your subject is 'The church at Ephesus,' " he informed me with formidable authority. I must confess that although I had spent most of my life in and around churches, I was not aware that they had a church in Ephesus, but I suddenly became an ardent student of that particular corner of "God's vineyard" (an expression I had heard preachers use).

My sole concern was to avoid making a fool of myself.

My motivation was less than honorable, of course. My sole concern was to avoid making a fool of myself, but I had an uneasy feeling that it would happen anyway.

The day arrived. A small group of young people gathered. They all wore slightly quizzical expressions as if they were wondering who I was and what I was doing. I had similar questions. Not daring to look at the people or the clock, I buried my nose in my notes, took a deep breath, and with trembling voice began. I knew I was supposed to have three points—I'm still not sure why! So I'd found three, the first one dealing with the church of Ephesus in Acts, the second in Ephesians, and the third in Revelation. In other words, I had prepared a brief summary of the New Testament. Eventually I stole a surreptitious glance at the clock. To my dismay I discovered I was already past finishing time and had only concluded my first point. I blurted, "I'm terribly sorry. I don't know how to stop." At that moment I was treated to a short lecture titled *Preaching 101.* An elderly gentleman who was apparently there to keep an eye on the proceedings said, "Shut up and sit down!" I did—hurriedly!

I assumed at that juncture that my preaching career had come to an ignominious end, and I found the thought strangely comforting. But no. The gentleman who had put me in the predicament in the first place bore down upon me and said firmly, "You didn't finish."

I responded meekly "no."

Then, to my horror, he added, "Then you'll come back next week and finish it!"

So I did, but I made sure I finished that time around, and with a great sense of relief I stepped down from the platform, ready to enjoy my well-earned retirement from preaching. Wrong again.

My tormentor told me, "There are lots of little Methodist churches around here, and they don't have preachers, so I've put your name on the Methodist circuit, and you will lead their services and preach for them." I inquired what I should do, and he pointed out that as I'd spent most of my life in church services up to that point, I should *know* what to do.

No Early Retirement

With that helpful advice carefully stored away, I embarked on something I'd had no intention of doing. Many Sunday afternoons found me pedaling my bicycle through the country lanes to picturesque Methodist chapels where a handful of godly farmers, having already done a day's work, were seated expectantly on hard benches. They had stoked up the wood-burning stove to inferno temperatures, eaten heartily, and squeezed themselves into the suits they'd been married in thirty years earlier. They were candidates for a Sunday afternoon snooze—and it was my job to deny them.

They loved the Lord, and they loved the Word, and they loved to hear it preached, and they wonderfully encouraged one shy, timid teenager who had been thrust reluctantly into their pulpit. "Aye, tha's right, lad," they would shout when I said something of which they approved. "Did you hear that?" they would ask one another, turning in the pews and punching one another awake. "Preach it, lad, preach it! Lord, help him to preach it!" And he did!

Discovering God's Gift

Something unexpected was happening to me. As I studied to teach, I discovered I was studying to learn. I was changing from a teenager who simply sat in church to a young man who was developing an appetite for God's Word. But there was more. I found that people wanted to listen to what I was discovering, and although I didn't know it at the time, I was unearthing a gift that God's Spirit had implanted in my life.

Harvest Festival was the big event in most of the Methodist churches I visited. The churches were beautifully decorated with colorful, fragrant produce that these hardworking sons and daughters of the soil had brought, and they exhibited a wonderful spirit of thanksgiving, praise, and gratitude to God, the one on whom they

> *As I studied to teach, I discovered*
> *I was studying to learn.*

———— ❦ ————

knew they were dependent. These events were so popular that some were held in huge barns. Even people who never went to church showed up. They sat on bales of hay, sang in wonderful harmony the great hymns of the faith to the accompaniment of the Salvation Army Band, and—amazingly—I was asked to preach at these "big" events. I began to wonder if I was a preacher or a banker.

Years later my work took me away from these wonderful country people to the great industrial city of Manchester. To mean streets, closed factories, unemployment lines, and hundreds of disillusioned, disgruntled, truculent teenagers. They gathered in coffee bars, and there they talked, drank, and listened to the Beatles, the Rolling Stones, and the Pretty Things. Some traded drugs, some engaged in teenage prostitution, and the rest just sat bored, waiting for something to happen. It did. My wife and I started to visit a coffee bar near our home called The Cat's Whisker. To our surprise we discovered that behind the long hair, grubby clothes, cynical attitudes, and question-able behavior, there were bright minds, inquiring spirits, and a zillion questions. As we talked to them, they gathered round, the music went unattended, someone shouted, "We can't hear you. Stand on a table!" And that's how a new approach to preaching developed. Night after night I stood on a table, preached a brief message, and answered ques-tions for an hour or two, then preached some more and answered more questions. Banking was definitely losing out to preaching!

Goodbye to Banking

Two or three years later, I left the banking business, and my wife and I joined a youth ministry called the Torchbearers. This ministry had been developed under the leadership of Major Ian Thomas, a deco-rated British Army officer, who at the end of World War II had started to work with young people in Germany. The work had flourished, and thousands of teenagers all over Europe were being reached with the good news. I joyfully joined in preaching to these young Europeans, and I found what I found everywhere else. People of all shapes and sizes are reachable through the preaching of the Word. Now it was Germans and Austrians, Swedes and Norwegians, Dutch and French, Swiss and Belgians, Danes and Finns—it didn't matter. The Word of God was relevant to all of them, and I was being asked to preach it!

I began to roam to other continents and eventually landed with my family on the shores of the U.S.A. I was called to pastor a church in Milwaukee, Wisconsin, the city Dwight L. Moody called "the grave-yard of evangelists."

Elmbrook church

I had greatly enjoyed and profited from the opportunities to preach around the world by this time, but I was concerned that I rarely had the chance to stay with people for an extended time to see the lasting effects of the preaching and to assist in its ongoing application. A pastoral heart was beating inside me, but I didn't know that was what it was called! As a banker-turned-preacher rather than a seminary-trained pastor, I never seriously expected to become a pastor. But I did, thanks to a brave group of people called Elmbrook Church who decided to gamble on this British banker who loved the Bible and had been encouraged to "Preach it!"

In December 2000 I completed thirty years as Elmbrook's senior pastor, celebrated my seventieth birthday, and, as it was the end of a millennium, concluded it was a good time to get out of the way. I explained to the church that I had no plans to retire or expire but planned to continue preaching around the world as I had done before coming to Elmbrook and had continued to do during the pastorate. So for the last three years, my wife and I have been operating as ministers at large on Elmbrook's staff, commissioned to go wherever we're invited, to encourage and help those whose task is to preach the Word. We've been on every continent except Antarctica, and wherever we go we find a hunger for truth and a readiness to listen—as well as a desire to preach the Word to those who need to hear it.

Wherever we go we find a hunger for
truth and a readiness to listen.

Learning Along the Way

My preaching call, practice, and experience are hardly standard—all right, they're abnormal—but along the way I've learned a few things about preachers and preaching that I've been asked to share with you. I've learned much about preaching from books, more from working with gifted preachers, and most from years of doing it. I owe so much to some wild, hairy kids in Manchester's coffee bars; to those European youngsters who survived World War II; to an enthusiastic group of Midwesterners who took a chance on a converted banker; and to a group of red-faced farmers in hot little chapels, who told me in broad North Country accents, "Preach it, lad, preach it!"

Young pastors and seminarians frequently ask me, "What advice would you give to someone starting out in ministry?" As they are often looking for a sound bite, I often reply, "Preach the Word and love the people." Obviously, many answers could be given to the question, but those who follow that advice will not go far wrong. Even so, ministry can be wearing, people can be difficult, and preaching regularly is not easy, so many preachers are looking for help and encouragement.

Barriers to Preaching

Part of the problem may be the discouragement occasioned by the steady flow of negative things about preaching that come the preacher's way from the church's detractors. Let's face it: Pulpits are not generally viewed with approval by many of our contemporaries. They are often seen as platforms for self-appointed bullies who have the arrogance and temerity to believe they know how other people should behave and are not at all reluctant to say so, loudly and clearly. In an environment in which anti-authority and pro-individuality attitudes prevail, it is not difficult to understand why preachers and preaching are not consensus favorites. In fact, a recent poll showed that a particular brand of preachers, namely televangelists, were rated among the top three "sleaziest" professions, along with mafia bosses and prostitutes. Standard dictionaries also project something of the public's disenchantment with preaching by defining the verb *to preach* as follows: "to give moral or religious advice, especially in a tiresome manner" (Webster's), and "to give advice in an offensive, tedious or obtrusive manner" (Chambers'). It's enough to tempt self-respecting preachers to hang up their lexicons.

We should not be surprised that church "outsiders" are not particularly enamored of preaching. After all, that's one big reason they're outsiders. But it does come as a surprise to discover a similar attitude among some church "insiders." Since the development of small groups within churches (which development I encourage), there have been, at best, a healthy discovery and implementation of scriptural truth in the lives of the participants, along with many other benefits. But at worst these meetings have been known to degenerate into little more than the pooling of ignorance and the endless repetition of real or imaginary ills, as the groups have moved away from any serious approach to the understanding and application of scriptural truth. In the same way, while there has been in some circles a new awareness of worship (which I applaud), the result has been a disproportionate emphasis on singing and "sharing" at the expense of teaching from the Word by able, gifted teachers. And, of course, the popularity and proliferation of concerts, to which the multitudes throng, are in marked contrast to the diminishing attendance at events specifically designed for the exposition of Scripture. These and other trends have led more than a few preachers to question the validity and effectiveness of preaching, and the result has been a marked loss of confidence in preaching.

Pulpits are not generally viewed with approval by many of our contemporaries.

In all fairness, some of the moves away from church events, where people were required to sit benignly at the feet of preachers, to more participatory activities have been most helpful, because people have learned more and done more as a result. Communication theorists insist people learn by listening, discussing, watching, and discovering. It must be conceded that preaching usually allows for only one or two of these methods. Considerations such as these have led respected Christian educators such as Dr. Lawrence O. Richards to say of preaching: "This form of communication has been shown most unlikely to change attitudes and values and consequently behavior. Preaching seldom leads to wholehearted response."

The Need for preaching

Our response to that should be to create ample opportunities for listening, discussing, watching, and discovering in the whole context of the church's life and ministry. There is no denying the validity and effectiveness of these things as means of learning. But neither dare we overlook the unique place of preaching in God's scheme of things and in the life of the church, for these reasons: Preaching assumes the uniqueness of the authoritative Word, the unique presence of the Holy Spirit as the Word is preached, the unique anointing and empowering of the preacher by the Spirit, and the unique activity of that same Spirit in the application of his inspired Word to the hearts of those who are receptive. With these factors in mind, it's clear that preaching is a form of communication unlike any other, and to compare preaching to other communication forms is to compare apples to oranges.

So while we warmly agree that there are many ways of communicating, we cannot agree that preaching is an ineffective way of doing it. God would not have made the basic error of telling us to use an ineffective method. And if preaching were ineffective, Jesus and the apostles would certainly have found a better way of getting their message across.

There is no shortage of modern-day preachers who testify to the remarkable work of grace through the preaching of the Word, which is evidenced in changed lives. Recently a young couple shyly introduced themselves to me after a Sunday morning service.

If preaching were ineffective, Jesus and the apostles would certainly have found a better way of getting their message across.

"We got married yesterday," they said.

"Great!" I replied. "I can highly recommend marriage."

"We wanted to tell you we've been living together for a couple of years, but when you preached on what the Bible says about sex a few weeks ago, we recognized our sin, repented, committed our lives to the Lord, got some counseling, and here we are—married!"

We all love to relate success stories like that. But as all preachers know, not everybody is listening to them, and many who give the impression that they are listening seem to have grown protective shields designed to prevent the message from penetrating deeply enough to effect noticeable change. Some people find listening to preachers tedious at best and irritating at worst. Geared as they are to visually oriented communication, their attention spans have become so seriously eroded that they find difficulty in concentrating and listening for more than a few minutes. This has led many preachers to look desperately for new ways to communicate the old message.

Then there is the matter of "felt needs." Subjected as they are to a constant bombardment of advertising, which skillfully exposes their innermost fears and ruthlessly exploits their inherent greed, modern people have started to believe it when they're told "You owe it to yourself." The self apparently is now owed a variety of things, most of which it has been persuaded to regard as needs whether or not they are simply whims or caprices, and all of which it believes must be satisfied as quickly, cheaply, and thoroughly as possible. So if the modern person is found in a pew, there's a very good chance he or she will have brought along a plethora of felt needs, which may or may not be

*In many churches there is a failure of
nerve where preaching is concerned.*

———————— ⟨◦/◦⟩ ————————

related to the deep, real needs of the soul, along with an expectation
that they will be met. Should the preacher not address these issues to
the listener's satisfaction and meet the corresponding expectations,
there is a real possibility that the message will be tuned out and the
plaintive cry "You didn't meet my needs" will be heard in the streets.

Let's face it: Preachers who have spent four of their best years and
thousands of dollars they don't have in a seminary learning about
supralapsarianism, Gnosticism, and hedonism may be reluctant to let
the investment go to waste. They may wish to share their discoveries
with the congregation, even if while they expound, Mrs. Smith is
wondering how to cope with her husband walking out and leaving her
with three kids and no rent money, and Mr. Jones, who has just discovered he is the codependent son of a passive-aggressive alcoholic who
produced a dysfunctional family, which accounts for his depression
and inability to cope with work, can't seem to get the preacher's drift.

stay the course

Because of these issues and others, in many churches there is a failure
of nerve where preaching is concerned. It is assumed that people will not
listen, they aren't interested, they can't concentrate. As a result, alternative
methods of communicating and participating, which may be perfectly
valid and helpful as *supplements* to preaching, have been installed as
substitutes for preaching. That makes no more sense than exchanging a
bottle of dietary supplements for a healthy diet of solid food.

Moreover, the preacher who has struggled to hold the line against
growing apathy or even antipathy toward preaching may be worn down,
discouraged, and even questioning the efficacy of preaching. This preacher
is in need of help. So let's see how we can encourage one another to
continue doing what the farmers said: "Preach it, lad, preach it!"

part 1
Preparing the Preacher

chapter ❷

The Preacher's Power Source

As we have seen, it is not difficult to understand why some preachers are looking for some encouragement in their ministry. But how to find it? Quite often, the tendency is to change methodology. The assumption is that if they can find a new technique or get ideas for new material, all will be well. They've heard about narrative preaching. That's a new idea. Maybe they should try that. They could even try dressing up like an Old Testament prophet. That might get people's attention for a couple of weeks. Or they've tried to do systematic exposition but got bogged down in Romans 9–11. It was great up to the end of chapter 8, but then they were not sure what to say, and the way the congregation's eyes glazed over during the last few weeks, it seemed they didn't want to hear it anyway. Maybe a dialogue sermon would help, but they're not sure what that is or how it works. Sounds intriguing but a little scary. Or what about tackling some "issues"? But which ones? And how many issues are there? So the search for new ideas continues, on the assumption that the new ideas will add power to the preaching.

It is perfectly possible that these preachers are right. But a word of caution: Before considering new techniques and ideas, it is advisable for preachers to first explore their own conditions. Are they feeling dry spiritually? Has preparation become boring? Do they enter the pulpit more with a feeling of dread than delight? Has preaching become a chore when once it was a calling?

Has preaching become a chore

when once it was a calling?

———— ❦ ————

Even with the best will in the world and the best ideas from the manuals, there is a limit to the effectiveness of preaching when it does not flow from a full heart and an overflowing spirit.

Busyness

When spiritual dryness attacks a preacher, it may be the result of downright disobedience, as evidenced by the all-too-frequent moral breakdown of preachers in recent years. But more often it is the result of busyness: well-meaning, good-hearted, earnest people who are too busy. Many preachers, particularly those who pastor small churches, are subject to enormous demands on their time: the expectations of their people, the multitude of tasks that need to be done, the shortage of volunteers to help with the work, the inadequacy of resources to increase efficiency. These all take their toll. As a result, pastors tend to busy themselves doing the things that cry loudest for their attention, which means that time for preparing both preacher and preaching gets whittled down to little or nothing.

Dennis Kinlaw wrote:

> Our perpetual temptation in the ministry is to let the ministry take priority over our personal walk with Christ. We are always conscious of the pressures to put the work first. That is so easy to justify. The reality, though, is that we always move from serving in His resources, gained from intimacy with Him, to ministry that arises from our strength alone.
>
> Our security against such a drift is the development of personal devotional habits that keep Him central and that maintain a perpetual influx of His life and power. We must know the resurrected Christ and commune with Him each day.[1]

My older son, David, was called to pastor a small church in the Upper Peninsula of Michigan. The week before he took up his responsibilities, he stayed with Jill and me in our home. This gave us a great opportunity to talk about the joys and tribulations of the ministry. I told him specifically that if he was going to minister to the people and care for his own spiritual nurture, he would need to discipline himself to set aside time for the study of the Word and personal devotion. He asked for suggestions as to how he could do this. So I told him to reserve, if possible, at least part of each morning for sermon preparation—and to remember the adage I had taught him from early days: "Never put your head on the pillow at night if you haven't had your nose in the Book during the day."

Our conversation was interrupted by a call from the church asking if he could arrive a day early because some of the men in the church were planning to fix an elderly church member's roof and they thought it would be good if the new pastor could be seen doing that kind of work. There is no doubt that this was a worthwhile endeavor and the PR, for a new pastor, would be invaluable. But I said to my son, "This is how it will be. There are so many good things to do and so many things you will be expected to do that you will struggle to preserve your own spiritual vitality, without which your ministry will dry up." Incidentally, he went a day early to work on the roof, but he took with him my parting advice: "By all means work on her roof, but when you stand before the people on Sunday morning, don't sound as if you've been on a roof all week."

———————— ⟨⟩ ————————

When spiritual dryness attacks a preacher, it
may be the result of downright disobedience,
but more often it is the result of busyness.

The Role of the Spirit

I find myself constantly returning to the scriptural passages in which Paul wrote autobiographically about ministry. One of the great biblical treasures for preachers is that we have not only a great amount of historical information concerning Paul's singularly effective ministry but also the autobiographical material which lifts the lid off his head and lets us see what made him tick. We not only know what he did, we are also aware of how and why he did it. His exploits are, no doubt, beyond the experience of us all. But the things that made him tick are so basic that all preachers would do well to study them carefully. They apply to every preacher who ever stood before people to open the Word. For example, he told the Corinthians: "My message and my preaching were not with wise and persuasive words, but with a demonstration of the Spirit's power, so that your faith might not rest on men's wisdom, but on God's power" (1 Corinthians 2:4-5).

There is no question about the apostle's brilliance, about his intellectual ability, about his considerable training. They are undeniable. But he insisted that the simple fact that he was highly trained and very bright and remarkably articulate would not guarantee the achievement of things of eternal consequence. He did not discount his gifts. They were clearly significant. God had built them into his life. They were all part of the package called Paul. But to be effective, his preaching needed much more, what he called "a demonstration of the Spirit's power." So it is with all preachers.

Opinions differ concerning the exact nature of the "demonstration" that attended Paul's preaching and what relevance, if any, it has today. There is no doubt that his apostolic preaching was reinforced by "signs and wonders," as was the preaching of both the prophets and the Messiah. The question upon which contemporary Christians cannot seem to agree is this: Given that the inception of prophetic, messianic, and apostolic preaching was attended by signs and wonders, can we and should we expect similar occurrences today? Or to put it another way: Can we really say that our preaching is effective if it is not backed up by signs and wonders? What can a modern-day preacher realistically expect

Never put your head on the pillow at
night if you haven't had your nose in
the Book during the day.

———— ❧ ————

to see that would confirm the preaching as a demonstration of the Spirit's power? Whatever our differences, I think all preachers would agree that minimally there should be evidence that the Word is taking root, that hearts are being changed, that minds are being renewed, that lifestyles are being revolutionized, that hearers are becoming doers, and people can see the difference. Using slightly different terminology, Richard Baxter, the seventeenth-century vicar of Kidderminster, said in his classic book *The Reformed Pastor* that preachers need the following:

> What skill is necessary to make plain the truth, to convince the hearers, to let in the irresistible light into their consciences, and to keep it there and drive all home. To screw the truth into their minds and work Christ into their affections...holy skill.[2]

We may not use Baxter's terminology, but we can certainly share his concerns and convictions. Making truth plain, convincing people, letting "irresistible light" into their consciences so effectively as to keep it there, and then to drive it all home and "screw the truth" into people's minds all sounds exciting and relevant and daunting. It requires power beyond rhetorical skill and the appeal of charismatic personality. So whether we talk about "holy skill" or "demonstration of the Spirit's power," it is clear that the preacher must be plugged in to a source of power other than purely human.

This power, while not unrelated to gifts and training and rhetorical skill, is totally different from them and infinitely superior to them. There is no shortage of communicators with all the skills of the rhetorical trade who make no eternal impact on people through their speaking. And there are men and women strangely lacking in what we would be

The preacher must be plugged in to a source of power other than purely human.

————— ⟨o∕o⟩ —————

inclined to regard as the necessary tools who exhibit a strange, compelling power in their preaching. Personally I think we should look for a combination of both, people who take the trouble to learn their trade and sharpen their skills *and* draw on the resources that only the indwelling Spirit provides. The work of convicting, convincing, and converting is the Spirit's, not the preacher's, and accordingly the preacher must learn to be the agent of the Spirit's working. This requires time and discipline, study and prayer, hunger and earnestness, dependence and obedience, expectancy and anticipation.

I have never yet met a preacher who was not interested in discovering power for preaching. But I have met a number who seemed, despite their interest, to overlook some basic truths. I do not say this in a critical spirit, for I was one of them. But fortunately I was helped as a young preacher to begin to realize the significance of Paul's words to the Ephesians: "I pray that out of his glorious riches *he may strengthen you with power through his Spirit* in your inner being" (Ephesians 3:16, italics added).

This power is related to the Spirit by whom each of the Ephesian Christians had been "marked with a seal" (Ephesians 1:13) and whom each one had received as a "deposit guaranteeing [their] inheritance" (Ephesians 1:14). Reading these verses, I came to the conclusion that if I was a Christian, I, too, had been sealed with the Spirit; he had entered my life to strengthen me with his power, and I should begin to live as if this were true. I read further that I should not "grieve" the Holy Spirit (Ephesians 4:30). The surrounding verses gave me plenty of instructions concerning this, and I was also aware that in the same way that men get drunk with wine, I was to go on allowing myself to be filled in my spirit by God's Spirit (Ephesians 5:18). Should this become my experience, I could then begin to count on being empowered by the

Spirit in grand style. Paul's doxology gave me some horizons that to this day I continue to delight in exploring: "Now to him who is able to do immeasurably more than all we ask or imagine, *according to his power that is at work within us,* to him be glory in the church and in Christ Jesus throughout all generations, for ever and ever! Amen" (Ephesians 3:20-21, italics added).

εxpecting the нoly spirit to act

I will never forget the sense of exhilaration that filled me as I began to preach, expecting the indwelling Spirit to be at work in and through the preaching. He who had inspired the Word I was trying to preach and who had promised to be present among the people to whom I was trying to preach could be counted on to bring to fruition that which was being sown. As I began to reckon with these truths, I became less self-conscious, less uptight, less concerned about how I was coming across, and even less interested in trying to produce results that would reduce my own insecurities. At the same time I became more relaxed, more reliant, more responsible, and more responsive in my own heart to what the Lord was saying to me long before I ever said it to anyone else.

People began to comment, including my own father and uncle, both of whom were venerable elders and seasoned lay preachers. They began to inquire how I gave the impression that I "expected something to happen." They said this not in an accusatory way but with winsome earnestness as they themselves began to testify to me, a young lay preacher in his early twenties, that they had never felt that joy or freedom. Since that time I have never felt free to look for other sources of power in preaching, for the simple reason that I am certain that I have not exhausted the resources of the indwelling Spirit by whom I was sealed for the day of redemption. From my perspective it would seem something of an insult to him to do anything other than that.

Paul went on to explain to the Corinthians that the power of God is seen to greatest advantage in human weakness. He was personally aware of this because the Lord had turned down his request to be delivered from his "thorn" and instead had told him, "My grace is sufficient for you, for my power is made perfect in weakness" (2 Corinthians 12:9).

Our spiritual power needs constant

attention through personal devotion.

———————— ❧❧❧ ————————

So Paul had determined to concentrate on knowing God and his grace
rather than concentrate on Paul and his problems, and in so doing he
had discovered the power not only to overcome his own difficult
circumstances but also the power to preach the message around the
Mediterranean region with an effectiveness that is unsurpassed to this
day. Paul reminds today's preachers that real preaching flows from
preachers who are powerful in a biblical sense.

Appropriating Grace

Sometimes we can be so busy preaching that we lose our cutting
edge. There is no shortage of effort; we keep on swinging our axes, but
instead of cutting through, we're simply bruising the bark. We need to
ask ourselves, "Where did I lose my cutting edge?" There is no question we were endowed with the Spirit when he entered our lives, and
there is no question that his power is available to us. But the edge has
gone. Where did it go? At what point did something alien enter our
lives that resulted in habit becoming sin, tiredness becoming slothful-
ness, busyness becoming coldness? When this happens, we need to
ask for the miracle of grace to restore the freshness of the Spirit. Then
we must reach out and appropriate it and start swinging all over again.
But this time with the cutting edge in place.

Like all cutting edges, our spiritual power can easily be blunted. It
needs constant attention through personal devotion. So before we look
for new methods to revive our flagging spirits or new techniques to revive
our waning enthusiasm, we need to check out the old masters such as
Paul who tells us, "My preaching [was] not with wise and persuasive
words, but with a demonstration of the Spirit's power" (1 Corinthians
2:4). Then we need to ask ourselves the searching question: "How
closely does my experience parallel that of the apostle?"

Endnotes

1. Dennis F. Kinlaw, *Preaching in the Spirit* (Grand Rapids, Mich.: Francis Asbury Press of Zondervan Publishing House, 1985), 22.

2. Richard Baxter, *The Reformed Pastor* (Edinburgh: The Banner of Truth Trust, first published 1656, reprinted 1989), 70.

I have not exhausted the resources of the indwelling Spirit by whom I was sealed for the day of redemption.

chapter ❸

....

Who Dares to Preach?

I've told you how I started preaching, and you may recall that I had little or no idea of what I was doing or what I was getting into. As time went by, I continued to tremble, not at the thought that I had to stand before a group of people and try not to disgrace myself, but rather at the thought that I was to stand in the presence of a holy God and explain his Word to people who needed to hear it. I began to ponder the question in the title of one of Wallace Fisher's books, *Who Dares to Preach?* This sense of preaching before the Lord hit home forcibly when I heard Billy Graham's answer to a reporter's question. As he stood outside the chapel at Sandringham, one of the queen's residences, after Sunday morning service, a reporter asked, "What's it like to preach before the queen?" Dr. Graham answered, "It's a great privilege, but you must remember, every time I preach I do so before the King of kings."

Preachers need to be careful about their preaching and even more careful about their living. Paul stated it this way: "By the grace God has given me, I laid a foundation as an expert builder, and someone else is building on it. But each one should be careful how he builds" (1 Corinthians 3:10).

Do I detect a note of proprietorship here? Was Paul saying, "That's my ministry you fellows are working on. Be careful. I put a lot of blood, sweat, and tears into that work. Don't mess it up!"? Probably not. His point appears to be that because Christ is the foundation that

The greatest care must be taken to ensure that nothing in the preaching detracts from the person of Christ or does damage to the message of the gospel.

———————— ⟨∽⟩ ————————

he has laid (he has preached Christ, and the people have responded), any further ministry of the gospel must be related to Christ himself in the same way that superstructures must be related to foundations. Therefore, the greatest care must be taken to ensure that nothing in the preaching detracts from the person of Christ or does damage to the message of the gospel. The old adage "If you can't be smart, be careful" is certainly appropriate for preachers.

There are at least three areas in which preachers must take great care. Paul clearly states (he is not speaking specifically of preaching but of ministry, which certainly includes preaching) that great care should be exercised in *how* we build. But it is clear that he is also concerned about *what* we build, and of course, *where* we build is of paramount importance.

HOW WE BUILD

"But each one should be careful how he builds" (1 Corinthians 3:10). A number of years ago, the church I serve embarked on a $12.5 million building extension. No doubt you will agree that is a lot of money, and I can assure you we did not embark on this enterprise lightly. Careful consideration was given to the necessity, the advisability, the viability, and numerous other "-ities" of the project before the concept was presented to the congregation. We considered all the reasons for and against before asking for a congregational decision. Then it was a matter of getting the financing, and there were many opinions as to how this should be done. But great care was exercised by our number crunchers to make sure the financing was handled properly. Then a building committee, composed of talented, hard-working people, was formed, and it began the most meticulous needs assessment (as opposed to wants assessment) and rigorous interviewing of prospective architects, builders, and subcontractors. Then the construction began. As the building progressed, I watched fascinated as men, working in frigid weather, erected 140-foot-long beams with the utmost accuracy required to make them fit to one-eighteenth of an inch. Great care was taken in every aspect of the building program. And rightly so. I can assure you that there was nothing shoddy about this piece of work, and I can say that because I managed to stay clear of the project. A wise move, given the tendency of pastors who get involved in building programs not to survive the experience.

How then should the preacher prepare to build? Phillips Brooks, in his famous lectures to Yale Divinity School students in 1877, said, "Let us rejoice with one another that in a world where there are a great many good and happy things for men to do, God has given us the best and happiest, and made us preachers of His truth."[1]

Notice the great sense of excitement and delight with which Brooks spoke of the ministry of preaching. Great care should be taken to preserve this sense of joy. But how is this to be done? Sometimes there is little visible response from the hearers. Sometimes there is a deadly sense of apathy or even outright resistance to the Word. Where, we might ask, is the joy in that kind of a situation? Surely it is to be found not in the measurable results but in the deep-rooted conviction that it is a joy to present truth in the midst of error and offer life in the place of deadness. Whether or not the hearers respond (or appear to

It is a joy to present truth in the midst of error and offer life in the place of deadness.

respond) is their responsibility. Giving them the chance to respond is the preacher's job and the preacher's joy.

But, even more significantly, the preacher preserves his or her joy in knowing that in the very proclamation of the truth God is being glorified. To think that the unsearchable riches of Christ can be presented by lips as weak and frail as ours and that finite words can exalt the infinite God is to experience deep joy even in the midst of discouraging circumstances.

Beware of depending on outward affirmation for your joy.

The story is told of John Wesley, who on one occasion was staying in an inn where a particularly raucous crowd was also staying. He was unable to sleep, so he went down among the men and preached to them through their drunken haze. They showed little interest in what he had to say, and some of them were outright antagonistic. When he had finished, one of Wesley's friends asked him what he had achieved, to which he replied that he had honored God in the proclamation of his truth and he had delivered his own soul from "blood guiltiness." If Wesley, on that occasion, had looked for his joy in the response of the drunks, he would have gone to bed miserable. However, he apparently found his delight in honoring God through his presentation of God's truth and felt that something of lasting worth had been achieved. Beware of depending on outward affirmation for your joy, and be careful to preserve your joy by remembering that God has given you "the best and happiest" of all the things you can be given to do.

We must also be careful not to lose sight of the solemnity and significance of the preaching event. The preacher is not only to be joyful in the preaching, but also earnest in the proclamation. It is perfectly possible, of course, for preachers to become "professional" in their approach to the preaching task. By that I do not mean that the preacher is wrong to utilize to the full his or her gifts and training, but that the preacher who has done it for so long may be prone to settle into the deep rut of dull routine. For such a person, preaching has become little more than a job to be done, a task to be accomplished. It is all too easy for the preacher to sit down to the mundane reality of churning out another talk and to stand before the people with an attitude of barely concealed boredom and frustration. Granted, there is much that is mundane about the work of preparing messages. It is work, and work can be arduous. But the preacher who truly does the work of ministry is always careful to preserve that unique sense of the real significance of the task. Richard Baxter, author of *The Reformed Pastor,* stated it with telling force:

> I preach'd as never sure to preach again,
>
> And as a dying man to dying men![2]

It may be objected that not all of us can maintain the kind of intensity that seventeenth-century preachers such as Baxter seemed to sustain. This may be a sad commentary on us and on our age. But the fact remains that the preacher who grips an audience is the preacher who is obviously gripped by the message. Care must therefore be exercised to see that the preacher demonstrates joy and intensity in the preaching. How he or she presents the message plays a major role in determining how it is received.

The preacher who grips an audience is the preacher who is obviously gripped by the message.

what we Build

Paul reminded the Corinthians also that they should be careful to examine *what* they built on the foundation he had laid. If I may return to our church building project for a moment, let me assure you that the quality of materials used was of prime concern. In the frigid temperatures we experienced during the building program, it was critically important that the welds on the great metal beams were made at the right temperature and that the right environment for cooling was in place. Each joint was carefully examined with X-ray and sonar devices to ensure the integrity of the welding, and I'm glad, because when I preach, I stand right under those beams. If they are not welded properly, they will make quite an impression on me when they come crashing down. "Be careful what you build" was the key phrase for our builders. Paul had similar ministerial concerns and put it this way: "If any man builds on this foundation using gold, silver, costly stones, wood, hay or straw, his work will be shown for *what* it is…the fire will test *the quality* of each man's work" (1 Corinthians 3:12-13, italics added).

This passage could legitimately be applied to the quality of preaching, but for now let us think about the quality of the preacher doing the presenting. We know that he is a sinner; we are aware that she is a fallen creature. But we also are aware that the ancient call of Isaiah for priestly ceremonial purity has its counterpart in contemporary ministry: "Depart, depart, go out from there! Touch no unclean thing! Come out from it and be pure, you who carry the vessels of the Lord" (Isaiah 52:11).

Given the swelling tide of lax contemporary morality and the alarming way in which it has eroded the pews and even undermined not a few of our pulpits, it is high time for a renewed call for moral purity among those who preach the Word. The words of the great apostle need to burn fiercely in the hearts of today's preachers:

> We have renounced secret and shameful ways; we do not use deception, nor do we distort the word of God. On the contrary, by setting forth the truth plainly we commend ourselves to every man's conscience in the sight of

God...What we are is plain to God, and I hope it is also plain to your conscience (2 Corinthians 4:2; 5:11).

"What we are" is something that preachers must be desperately careful to preserve. Baxter again puts it well:

> O brethren, watch therefore over your own hearts; keep out lusts and passions, and worldly inclinations; keep up the life of faith, and love and zeal...Above all, be much in secret prayer and meditation. Thence you must fetch the heavenly fire that must kindle your sacrifices.[3]

where we Build

Finally, great care must be taken concerning *where* we build. Note Paul's assumption: "I laid the foundation and someone else is building on it." Every preacher worth his or her salt knows that Christ is the foundation of all that God is doing in the lives of men and women today. But the preacher is subtly tempted to be less than careful about where the superstructure of life is erected after the foundation has been laid. At the risk of stating the obvious, Paul quite naturally assumes that those who follow up his ministry will build upon that which he laid. Or, to put it another way, they will continue in the things that they have initially learned. Should we be tempted to assume that people would not be stupid enough to build away from the foundations, we should remember that Paul found it necessary to rebuke the Galatians for "so quickly deserting the one who called [them]" (Galatians 1:6). He also found it necessary to remind Timothy to "continue in what you have learned and have become convinced of" (2 Timothy 3:14). And to the Colossians he wrote, "So then, just as you received Christ Jesus as Lord, continue to live in him, rooted and built up in him, strengthened in the faith as you were taught and overflowing with thankfulness" (Colossians 2:6-7).

Strange as it may seem, it is not uncommon for preachers to become so casual in the ministry that they fail to recognize their drift away from their basic commitment to Christ in their spiritual lives and their diminishing trust in Christ in ministry. Let me be specific. It is much more likely that the preachers who are concerned about preaching problems will turn to a book on the techniques of preaching (which may be very helpful) or attend a seminar on the latest trends in preaching (which may be very insightful) before they turn inward to see if there is any deficiency in their relationship with the One who is the foundation of all that they know and all that they have. It is not unusual for modern preachers, in other words, to give insufficient attention to the possibility that they are building at some distance from their foundations.

Errol Hulse wrote:

> Our concern is to derive from Christ the spiritual power to live holy lives and to preach powerful sermons. The one is the support, pillar, and foundation of the other. This power can only be enjoyed as we abide in Christ. That means maintaining an intimate sharing partnership with the person of Christ continually.[4]

Recently my wife and I ministered at the Beeson International Center for Biblical Preaching and Church Leadership, a branch of Asbury Theological Seminary. We spoke to crowded chapels full of sharp young people from forty nations who are investing years in preparation for ministry and service. They expressed appreciation for the Word of the Lord that had come to their hungry hearts. They testified to the specific relevance of the sermon to their situations, and I realized all over again how hungry people are for truth and how eagerly they come to worship expecting to hear a word from the Lord. And that was once again a reminder to me to be careful in my life and ministry. Too much depends on it for me to be careless.

We are dealing with real people and real issues. People have real problems and are looking for sharp, clear, life-giving truth. This is serious business, and that means we have to take it seriously and ensure that we are careful to be powerful.

Powerful and *careful* are the operative words we have considered so far. Now let's turn our attention to what it means to be *faithful.*

I must be careful in my life and ministry.

Too much depends on it for me to be careless.

Endnotes

1. Phillips Brooks, *The Joy of Preaching* (Grand Rapids, Mich.: Kregel Publications, 1989), 25.

2. *The Oxford Dictionary of Quotations* (Second Edition, London: University Press, 1941), 36.

3. Richard Baxter, *The Reformed Pastor* (Edinburgh: The Banner of Truth Trust, first published 1656, reprinted 1989), 62.

4. Samuel T. Logan, Jr., ed., *The Preacher and Preaching* (Phillipsburg, N.J.: Presbyterian and Reformed Publishing Company, 1986), 87.

chapter ❹

Faithfulness Required

Paul had much more to say concerning his own approach to ministry:

> So then, men ought to regard us as servants of Christ and as those entrusted with the secret things of God. Now it is required that those who have been given a trust must prove *faithful* (1 Corinthians 4:1-2, italics added).

Faithful to what? Paul had at least two roles in mind. First, he called himself a servant of Christ, and second, he stated that he should be regarded as one "entrusted with the secret things of God." Both roles can easily be seen as opportunities either for the abuse of privilege or for committed and effective service. For both roles to be appropriately discharged requires great faithfulness.

Huperetes

In the expression "servant of Christ," Paul used the word *huperetes* (servant) instead of the more common word *doulos*. It means literally "one who assists the principal in the fulfilling of his objectives." It is used, for instance, to describe John Mark who traveled along with Paul and Barnabas until he quit, and they subsequently argued over him and went their separate ways. He is described in the King James Version as "their minister," which could be misleading because he actually went along as their assistant. Paul and Barnabas called the shots, and he was the expediter. So presumably he saw to the mundane

There's a phenomenal sense of privilege in
being called to preach—and great care must
be taken not to lose that sense of privilege.

tasks of ministry as he fixed their itineraries, hired their donkeys, and made their reservations.

Huperetes is also used in Jesus' teaching. He said that if someone sues you, it is advisable to settle out of court rather than run the risk of having the judge find against you and deliver you over to the "jailer" (huperetes). If you aren't careful, you might get a little convoluted at this point and conclude, "So men ought to regard us as jailers of Christ," which, of course, is putting two and two together and coming up with five. No, the point here is that the jailer does not determine the sentence. The judge does, and the jailer is simply the one who assists the principal in the fulfilling of his objective.

I am particularly interested in the use of *huperetes* in secular Greek where it means literally "under-rower." Try to imagine a boat plying the Mediterranean. On the upper deck stands the captain, and he determines *where* and *when* the boat will sail. On the lower deck are ranks of people whose sole responsibility is to pull on the oars when they are told. They are clearly assisting the principal in fulfilling his objective. They are under-rowers.

By using this term, Paul gives a graphic and dramatic insight into his perception of ministry. As far as he is concerned, he does not proclaim ideas of his own in his preaching. Neither does he formulate and propagate his own agenda. What he actually does is speak in such a way that he might assist the principal in the fulfilling of his objective. His principal is Jesus Christ. He recognizes that Jesus wants to say something. He recognizes that Jesus wants to do something. He realizes that Jesus has something to proclaim to Corinth. Paul sees his responsibility perfectly clearly. It is to pull on the oars so that what Jesus has to say might be heard and what Jesus wants to do might be accomplished in the desperately needy city of Corinth. To me that is an exciting picture.

More than thirty-three years ago, God in his wisdom called my wife and me to Milwaukee, Wisconsin. Up until that time we really didn't know that Milwaukee, Wisconsin, existed. But God brought us out of England and deposited us in that city.

As soon as word got out that we were planning to go, we received all kinds of really encouraging responses from people. A close friend on the Billy Graham team called me and said, "Stuart, do you realize that Milwaukee, Wisconsin, is the biggest city in America to which Billy Graham has never been invited?" Somebody else called from the Moody Bible Institute to tell me, "Stuart, do you realize that Dwight L. Moody said Milwaukee is the graveyard of all evangelists?" And Alan Redpath called me and said, "Stuart, you should reconsider. I've preached around the world, and I want to tell you that two of the worst weeks of my life were spent in Milwaukee, Wisconsin."

With this encouragement, we moved to Milwaukee. Shortly afterward, I was flying home with a friend, Willy, in his light aircraft. We were coming in late at night, and we could see the great city of 1.25 million people below us. I said to my friend, "Let's just circle the city." As we were flying around, I asked him, "What do you see?"

He said, "I see Old Milwaukee."

"What else do you see?" I asked.

He replied, "I know what you want me to say. You want me to say that there's a city Jesus wants to touch."

"Yes," I answered, "I have the strangest feeling that for some reason God in his wisdom wants us to invest ourselves in this city, to pull on the oars, because there's something he wants to say and there's something he wants to accomplish there." Unfortunately Willy, who shared the vision, died in a fiery crash of his aircraft shortly afterward. But thirty-two years later, we're still pulling on the oars in Old Milwaukee!

There's a phenomenal sense of privilege in being called to preach—to bring the unsearchable riches of Christ to a certain place—and great care must be taken not to lose that sense of privilege. When you under-stand and sense that privilege, the call then is to be faithful to that privileged position, to be the *huperetes* of Jesus Christ.

mysterion

Then Paul talked about being "entrusted with the secret things of God." The King James Version, with typically majestic, albeit anti-quated, language, uses the expression "stewards of the mysteries." Isn't that delightful? "Stewards of the mysteries" rolls off the tongue, which is one of the nice things about Old English—for an old Englishman, anyway. It gives a sense of appropriate dignity that "those entrusted with the secret things of God" doesn't quite preserve… although it must be admitted that it preserves this dignity at the risk of ambiguity.

The word translated "mystery" in the King James Version and "secret things" in the New International Version is *mysterion.* Paul liked to talk about *mysterion,* and it is important that we get a sense of what he meant. *Mystery* and *secret things* don't do justice to his meaning, because our modern understandings of the terms differ dramatically from his understanding. In common parlance a mystery or a secret is something obscured or hidden, and in the specialized sense of an Agatha Christie mystery, it is something confusing.

My wife loves to read Agatha Christie novels. I don't. She finds them exciting, and I find them boring. I contend that they are all more or less the same. They start off with about ten or twelve people stuck in a train or a hotel with no way out. The first chapter describes the people, all of whom are quite beautiful, with the glaring exception of one, who is a real creep. At the end of the first chapter, somebody is found dead. Who "dunnit"? The creep, of course. So why read the rest of the book? In the next chapter, however, you discover that one of those apparently very nice people was really not very nice at all. When, at the end of the second chapter, the creep of the first chapter is found very dead, you say, "Aha! It must have been the second person, who at first seemed very nice." And so it goes for twelve chapters until in the end everybody is bumped off, you are convinced Mrs. Christie has been trying to confuse you, and you conclude she must have done it herself. It seems to me that this is how mysteries work, which is not particularly important until we realize that some people subconsciously think the God who deals in mysteries must in some way resemble a celestial Agatha Christie, sitting up there in his heaven, spinning events likely to confuse.

Accordingly, some people have simply copped out on the mysteries of God, assuming that God is some sort of mystery writer in the sky who has the most wonderful time confusing us and that we should not make any attempt to figure out what is going on. Now that is absolutely not what Paul meant by mysteries and secrets.

Paul borrowed a term from the mystery religions, which proliferated in his day, and used it to communicate with his contemporaries. They understood that in the mystery religions there were certain secrets that were hidden to the uninitiated but revealed to the initiated. So if you were initiated, you were let in on the secret, and if you were uninitiated, you were in the dark. Paul was simply saying, "Guess what! God in his infinite grace has touched my life. He who commanded light to shine out of darkness has shone in my heart and has given me the knowledge of God in the face of Jesus Christ, and, incredible as it seems, he has revealed to me things of which I, in my uninitiated, unconverted days, was totally ignorant. And not only that, I now realize I am totally surrounded by people who are living in the dark, while God has opened *my* eyes to allow me to live in the light." That's what it means to be alerted to the mysteries, and that is what has happened to the redeemed child of God.

In what way should this have an impact on the preacher? There are several answers, but I will concentrate on only one. Let's look again at the idea that those who have been initiated are in the light as opposed to those who are uninitiated and in the dark. I have been particularly impressed by the depth of the darkness in which people around me live. I recognize that even to say this smacks of arrogance, but, on the other hand, *not* to say it smacks of impertinence in the sense that not to say it is in some way to deny what God has said and done. So let us humbly accept that, for reasons attributable only to divine grace, we

Some people live their lives purely on the basis of speculation.

have been ushered into the light, and round about us are those who are living in the dark. What does this mean?

I look at it this way. Some people live their lives purely on the basis of speculation. They periodically confront the real-life issues by asking questions such as "Who am I? Where did I come from? Why am I here? Where am I going?" Then they begin, with or without the help of friends, families, or professors, to guess at the answers: "Well, I think I evolved from something; I believe that when you're dead you're finished; I believe life is a bowl of cherries; I think that if you live a good life, you go to heaven when you die." But they are all guesses. This is pure speculation, and it is what people do all the time.

In marked contrast to this approach is what I will call, for want of a better term, revealed theology. The difference between speculative philosophy and revealed theology is stark. The former is man's best shot (to give him the benefit of the doubt) at getting the big answers to the big questions right, and the latter is God's authoritative word on the basic issues. In the former approach, man sits on a rock, scratches his bald spot, and with furrowed brow puzzles his way to uncertainty. In the latter he is required to sit down, be quiet, and listen to what God has to say on the subject. And that involves not only answers to the questions man tends to ask, but also answers to the big question he may not have been concerned to ask, and that is "Who is God?" In fact, none of the man-centered questions can be answered adequately without their being God-centered. If man's man-centered questions find only man-centered answers, confusion is inevitable. But if God-centered questions bring about God-centered answers that lead to life, how great is the privilege of the one whose eyes have been opened to revealed theology and to the mysteries! And how vast is the privilege that is his or hers to be a dispenser of a God-centered message to a confused society!

But notice something else. Once I am alerted to the mysteries, it is not so that I might revel in my initiated position or that I might rejoice in the fact that my blind eyes have been opened. It is that I might be a steward of those mysteries, or someone entrusted with the secret things.

oikonomos

A steward *(oikonomos)* was someone who was put in charge of the estate and servants of the master on the understanding that he would exercise his responsibilities in such a way that the master's interests would be well cared for. The *oikonomos* was perfectly free to enjoy the materials that were placed under his jurisdiction, but they never belonged to him, and he was ultimately responsible to give an account of his stewardship.

When people came into the bank where I worked and handed over their money to me, I never thought for a moment that it was being delivered to me in any other capacity than as "steward." When they returned and asked for it, I handed it over to them without any argument. They, of course, would have been outraged if I had misappropriated the funds and had failed to return them on demand. That would have been the ultimate failure on my part, because, as Paul wrote, "It is required that those who have been given a trust must prove faithful" (1 Corinthians 4:2).

So Paul's emphasis was perfectly clear. As a *huperetes* and an *oikonomos,* he was placed by God, in accordance with his master plan, in a position of great privilege and responsibility, and his mandate was to faithfully discharge his responsibilities and to be accountable for the trust placed in him. So it is with those who take up the preaching task today.

So according to Paul, an effective minister of the gospel is characterized by a life that is powerful, careful, and faithful. But Dr. Martyn Lloyd-Jones shall have the last word. He put it this way:

An effective minister of the gospel
is characterized by a life that is
powerful, careful, and faithful.

———— ⟨✿⟩ ————

What matters? The chief thing is the love of God, the love of souls, a knowledge of the Truth, and the Holy Spirit within you. These are the things that make the preacher. If he has the love of God in his heart, and if he has a love for God; if he has a love for the souls of men, and a concern about them; if he knows the truth of the Scriptures, and has the Spirit of God within him, that man will preach.[1]

"The doctor," as Lloyd-Jones was affectionately known, had very definite and unmistakably articulated views on many things, and not everyone agreed with him all the time. But I never met anyone who, having heard him preach, suggested he was less than a superb preacher. Even in his waning years, there was always plenty of power in the pulpit he occupied. We do well, therefore, to mark carefully his words and note what, according to him, will ensure "that man will preach." It is the powerful, careful, faithful preacher who delivers a compelling word from the throne—and sends people on their way from the preaching event refreshed, renewed, and ready to serve.

Endnote

1. D. Martyn Lloyd-Jones, *Preaching and Preachers* (London: Hodder and Stoughton, 1971), 120.

chapter ⑤

....

Preaching Under Pressure

Having stated his convictions about ministry, and having conveyed his great sense of privilege in being called to be a *huperetes* and an *oikonomos,* Paul went on to speak realistically about the things in his life that could have militated against his faithfully fulfilling his mission. He told the Corinthians quite frankly, "I care very little if I am judged by you or by any human court; indeed, I do not even judge myself. My conscience is clear, but that does not make me innocent" (1 Corinthians 4:3-4).

I would love to have been a fly on the wall of the Corinthian church when those words were read out to the assembled saints! Don't forget that some of them were less than impressed with Paul in general and with his ministry in particular. So his statement concerning their view of him and his view of their view of him might not have set too well in some of the pews. But our concern is not with their view of Paul. We need to look into the factors Paul hinted at that could have been major deterrents to faithful ministry, because, strange as it may seem, they still exist to this day in the modern preacher's situation. We need to be aware of them because if they are not recognized promptly and dealt with summarily, they can have an erosive effect on the preacher.

Paul had clearly shown his great sense of privilege in ministry, but then he turned to a consideration of the pressures on the preacher. It's very important that we understand this, because sometimes the pressures can become so great that all sense of privilege dissipates. Like the man who was tarred and feathered and was heard to say, "If it weren't

*Sometimes the pressures can become so
great that all sense of privilege dissipates.*

———————— ⟨⟨⟩⟩ ————————

for the honor of this thing, I'd just as soon not go through with it,"
there are preachers who, having been figuratively tarred and feathered,
have forgotten the honor of their situation and have therefore preferred
not to go through with it. That is why I have emphasized the
preacher's privilege. But let's face it: There are very real pressures, too.

pressure points

Paul does not specify the pressures to which he was subjected, but
they are clearly implied, so we can legitimately infer what they were. First,
he talked about being "judged by you." In other words, he was aware that
he was being subjected to critical evaluation by the Corinthian congregation. Then he mentioned being judged "by any human court." This is an
interesting expression. From the Greek it literally means "man's day." I
assume he was talking about "man's day" or "the day of man" in marked
contrast to "the day of the Lord," which he certainly had in mind in this
passage. The day of the Lord is the time of ultimate evaluation by the
Lord, who knows the end from the beginning and has the unique ability
rightly to discern and evaluate the motives of people's hearts. In dramatic
contrast to the day-of-the-Lord evaluation is the day-of-man, or man's-
day, evaluation. This, rather than being divine, is purely human; rather
than being ultimate is immediate; and rather than being eternal is simply
contemporary. And so it would seem to me that Paul implied he was
being critically evaluated not only by the congregation in Corinth but also
by contemporary society. But then notice the third pressure we can infer
he was experiencing. He said, "I do not even judge myself." He was
talking about personal pressure. So we can see that the three pressure
points for Paul and for many a modern-day preacher—that can rob us of a
sense of privilege and take the freshness out of our pulpits—are congregational, societal, and personal.

congregational pressures

First let us consider what Paul referred to when he said, "I care very little if I am judged by you." It is clear he was coming under some kind of congregational pressure. Congregations vary considerably, but I suspect that all preachers come under some kind of congregational pressure at one time or another. Depending on the nature of the pressure and the temperamental and spiritual health of the preacher, the pressure may or may not be totally debilitating.

Congregational pressure comes in a variety of forms. Paul's problem apparently stemmed from the fact that the Corinthians had their own ideas of what he should be doing as far as their church was concerned, and apparently what they had in mind for him did not equate with what he himself was convinced God had called him to do. So, for instance, when he started to preach to them about sexual ethics and normative sexual behavior for Christians, it quickly became apparent that they and he were not even on the same page. He was appalled at the lax standards with which they were perfectly comfortable, and when he attempted to rectify what he saw as grave aberrations of Christian behavior, he encountered resistance. In other words, there were those at Corinth who preferred to do it their way rather than hear about doing things God's way. So what's new?

All preachers come under some kind of congregational pressure at one time or another.

pressure from intimidators

Now I realize we may be on thin ice at this point, but let's skate on it anyway. Remember that Paul was in Corinth to be an under-rower of Jesus Christ and as one entrusted with the secret things of God, which,

It is not uncommon to find churches
in which people are totally
committed to the status quo.

———————— ◈ ————————

we have seen, also describes the role of the modern preacher. So let's look at his situation and see how it relates to the situations preachers face in today's churches.

It is not unusual for a preacher to come into a church desiring only to be a powerful, faithful, and of course, careful preacher of the gospel. Unfortunately, when he sets about the task, he discovers that the congregation isn't terribly interested in such high-sounding concepts. They had given the preacher a very high-sounding job description, and the search committee had come out with a wonderful picture of the church. But when tested, their description soon began to look more like the work of the Junior Chamber of Commerce. However, the preacher has arrived wanting to communicate the Word and apply it to the life of the believers and the culture in which they live. But the congregation is on a different wavelength. For instance, it is not uncommon to find churches in which people are totally committed to the status quo. "As it was in the beginning, is now and ever shall be, world without end" is their motto. The more the preacher tries to preach the Word, the more he or she discovers that the status is exceedingly quo.

But when the Word is preached in power, progress is one of the inevitable results. And there is no such thing as progress without change, but change and status quo mix like oil and water. So a difficult situation emerges. What is a preacher to do?

On the one hand is pressure to conform to what the congregation wants. And let's face it: They pay the bills! If they don't like what he says, he is history, out of work, gone without severance pay. On the other hand, his whole point in being there is to be faithful. He is convinced something needs to be said or something needs to be done, but it might step on toes—big toes, like those of the chairman of the board.

Granted, the following is an extreme example, but it will serve to make the point. What happens if the preacher feels he should preach from 1 Thessalonians and he comes to chapter 4, verses 3-6: "It is God's will that you should be sanctified: that you should avoid sexual immorality; that each of you should learn to control his own body in a way that is holy and honorable, not in passionate lust like the heathen, who do not know God; and that in this matter no one should wrong his brother or take advantage of him"—but there are reasons to believe that Brother Deep Pockets has not been as strict about this as Scripture says he should?

If he starts preaching what Paul told the Thessalonians, the preacher will really put the cat among the pigeons, as we say in England. The preacher may be tempted to back off. He doesn't want to rock the boat or muddy the waters, so he rationalizes, "None of us is perfect, and maybe a different series would be more suitable." It's the pressure of intimidation, a very real pressure, and the trouble is that if preachers succumb to it, the first casualty of intimidation is faithfulness.

A young preacher who started his ministry in Kentucky preached his first sermon on the evils of smoking, only to be informed by the deacons that a third of the members made their living growing tobacco. So the following week he addressed drinking and was told that a third of the people made bourbon. The third week he explained the dangers of betting on the horses and was informed that the other third of his congregation did not appreciate what he had said because they bred thoroughbred horses. So, finally getting the message, on the fourth week

———— ⸙ ————

The first casualty of intimidation
is faithfulness.

he preached on the dangers inherent in deep-sea fishing in international waters. Now that's playing it safe. It is also succumbing to intimidation.

pressure from adulators

You will notice that factions had developed in the Corinthian church that had, not surprisingly, fragmented the fellowship. The church members had developed their own preferences concerning church leaders and without apology had become known as followers of different men. They had apparently identified themselves by taking the names of their favorite preachers; so one group said they followed Paul—the Paulines; another Apollos—the Apollines; and the others Cephas—the Cephites. Then there were the ones who simply said they were following Christ—the Christians; they were the "supersaints," I suppose.

You'll notice that Paul had his own following. And in every congregation, however tough it gets, the pastor usually has his own following, even if it is only his wife, his mother, and in some rare instances his mother-in-law. By no means would I ever begrudge a pastor a cheering section—a support group. It is needed. But unfortunately it can create a special kind of problem, a new kind of pressure. It is the pressure of adulation.

A little lady named Jennie Hext lived a couple of doors away from us some time ago. Early one morning as I drove past her driveway, I saw her shoveling snow. I had a little time before my breakfast meeting, so I went to help this elderly lady. Her response to my offer was "Don't you waste your time shoveling my drive. You just get on with what you do. I can shovel a driveway. In fact, I was trying to get mine done so I could come and do yours. You just get on with what you're doing."

Then she told me what she used to tell me every time I saw her. "Old Steve [her husband] and I went to church all our lives, and we never knew that we needed Jesus, and we never knew that Jesus could come into our lives and turn our lives around. Someone dragged us into that church where you preached one time. One Sunday did it. I don't know what is happening in all these other places. I don't know what those guys are talking about. All I know is, you know how to tell it. So you get

The preacher may give more attention

to keeping the cheering section cheering

than to preaching the Word faithfully.

out there and tell 'em, and I'll shovel my own drive and yours as well."
To reinforce her point, she waved her snow shovel in the air and added,
"By the way, I hear that some of the people in that church are giving
you a hard time. Listen, you just tell 'em from me what I just told you.
Tell them this: Just a short time after old Steve and I came to your
church, he died, and you buried him, and he went to heaven. Where
would he have been if you hadn't told us? As far as I'm concerned, if
you say it, it's right, and if any of those people give you any more
trouble, send them to me." With that she made a great sweeping movement with her snow shovel, and I have to confess that I had a mental
picture of a number of people I'd like dear Jennie to minister to.

But there is danger lurking beneath this affirming surface. It's not
only the danger of believing what your fans say about you, but it also
has to do with the very real possibility that the preacher may give more
attention to keeping the cheering section cheering than to preaching
the Word faithfully. Everyone can handle a little affirmation, and there
isn't always enough to go around. So whenever there is any to be had,
the tendency is to make sure it keeps coming. But the focus can too
easily be diverted from preaching the Word faithfully to keeping the
adulators adulating.

If the danger of the pressure of intimidation is that it can tie your
hands, the trouble with adulation is it can swell your head.

pressure from Agitators
Not only was there a party whose members said, "I follow Paul," but
as we have already pointed out, there were also those whose rallying
cry was "I follow Christ." Now I hope I am being fair to those people,

but I rather suspect they thought they were above all the partisan business and were spiritually superior, and they had no compunction about saying so. They were living in a sort of celestial stratosphere.

My experience—and most pastors with whom I have talked on the subject confirm it—is that it is not uncommon to find similar groups in our churches to this day. Good people who are serious, earnest, and devout, but difficult. I call them supersaints. When they come to talk to you, they have a very serious look (bordering on sour) on their faces. They have a habit of prefacing their opinions with "The Lord told me" or "The Lord said to me." But then it can get very embarrassing. After they've told you what the Lord has said to them, they say, "But what do you think?" That immediately puts you on the ropes, doesn't it? "The Lord said this to me, but what do you think?" How can you possibly disagree with what they think, when they have already informed you that it is what the Lord has said? Somehow or other they have got an inside track with the Lord, and you are left out there on the rails.

I've occasionally tried a little humor at that point. "Well, if he's for it, I'm against it." That approach is ill-advised; it has never worked. They are usually so earnest that they are rarely humorous. They are too busy being spiritual. So I've tried to engage them in conversation.

"What was that you said?"

"The Lord told me."

"When did he do that?"

"Well, as I was waiting on him this morning."

"What time was that?"

"Seven-thirty."

"Hmm. That's funny."

"What's funny about that?"

"Well, I was just talking to him, and he never mentioned it to me."

That doesn't work either!

One of the biggest shocks of my early pastoral ministry was to discover that a group in the church whom I regarded as some of the most devoted and effective people, and who actually prayed as I was speaking, were not what I thought they were. Some members of the church, much more astute than I was (and am), went to them and said, "What's the problem? You sit in the worship service looking as if you're sucking lemons. Why don't you either join us or ship out? You make us feel bad just looking at you."

They replied, "The Lord has told us to stay here until we have prayed Briscoe out of this place! He is the worst thing that ever happened to this church." Subsequently I discovered that while I was speaking they were praying, "Oh, Lord, get him out of here!" Now that's hard to take!

Agitators break your heart, while intimidators tie your hands, and adulators swell your head. By the time you've dealt with all these pressures, it may just escape your mind that you are there to be faithful. And therein lies the problem.

Agitators break your heart, while intimidators tie your hands, and adulators swell your head.

chapter ⑥

....

More Pressure for the Preacher

As if congregational pressure were not enough to cope with, there is more. Paul implied, as we saw in the last chapter, that he was also subjected to pressure from "man's day," or, as we interpreted it, from contemporary secular society.

Of course, in many parts of the world, total freedom to preach the gospel as we enjoy it does not exist. Preachers are placed under specific restrictions to which they must adhere or face the consequences, and recent church history is replete with examples of men and women who did just that. Some languished in prisons for years rather than identify with regimes that would render their ministries ineffective and would require them to be less than faithful. Others, with great demonstrations of ingenuity, found ways in which to obey the letter of the law and at the same time make room for the kind of ministry to which they had been called. They carried on their ministries and stayed out of jail, but only by the skin of their teeth.

On more than one occasion I have been invited to speak in churches that were under the baleful eye of totalitarian Marxism. I was informed that I was not licensed to preach and therefore could not do anything other than bring greetings. It was suggested to me with a deadpan expression and a twinkle in the eye that the greetings should take about an hour, and then the pastor would deliver the closing message, which as it turned out usually lasted a couple of minutes. In each case there was a refusal to allow the contemporary society to call the shots of the preacher's ministry, however hard it tried.

pressure of politics

Things are completely different for those of us who minister in the free world. Nevertheless, I am not unaware that congregations can come under pressure from secular society in the form of local government when, for instance, they want to erect new buildings or expand their existing facilities. As a result, they may find themselves in the middle of local politics. Recognizing the quid pro quo way of doing things in the political arena, the preacher can easily be pressured into deals that "don't smell too good" outside the church council chamber, or even into muting necessary statements concerning certain activities in which the government is involved and in which some local political heavyweights have more than a passing interest. Better not twist their tails, or they might gobble up the whole project.

Many preachers in the Western world never feel any particular pressure from this source. They have carved out reasonably comfortable situations in which to conduct their ministries. They don't feel any particular necessity or even urgency to address the secular society in which they live, other than to condemn it from the security of the sanctuary—and then only to those with whom they are in tacit, if not total, agreement. As a result, a state of evangelical detente prevails. Provided the church ignores and leaves the secular society alone, the society will reciprocate. But this is hardly the stuff of which "salt and light" are made.

Provided the church ignores and leaves the secular society alone, the society will reciprocate. But this is hardly the stuff of which "salt and light" are made.

Congregations vary in their stands on the church's role in relation to the state. Church history shows clearly how the church's stance has altered in different eras and under differing regimes. But Paul, even though he spoke warmly of the role of the government of his day and benefited from its protection more than once, was still careful to insist that if the secular society put him under the gun so that his faithful presentation of the Word was jeopardized, he would have none of it. Whatever the pressure and from whatever source it came, he was committed to being faithful.

pressure of Relevance

Perhaps the biggest pressure point for modern pastors in the Western world comes not so much from the political arena as from their concern to be relevant. This, of course, is a most noble desire, and it is hard to see how a ministry can be justified if it is not married to relevance. But being relevant and being pressured by secular society are closely related. For example, any modern preacher who is remotely aware of contemporary society's interests will endeavor to capitalize on them. It is clear that people are more likely to listen to that which interests them than to that which bores them. And by the same token, they are much more likely to respond to that which they believe will help them than to that which simply informs them of irrelevancies. If they aren't listening, talking won't achieve much.

But what if a great gulf is fixed between people's interests and what God wants to say to them? Should preachers see any attempt to get on society's wavelength as a temptation to compromise? Obviously not! But how far should they go in catering to the interests of the secularists to communicate the good news to them? And at what point are they in danger of being less than faithful to the message delivered to them? It gets tricky when preachers have to begin to wonder if they must choose between being faithful and being relevant. The dichotomy exists only in the preacher's mind, of course, but the pressure is real nevertheless. We'll talk more about this later, but right now it serves our purposes, by way of illustration, to identify this as a source of genuine pressure for the modern preacher.

What if a great gulf is fixed between people's interests and what God wants to say to them?

———— ⤙⟡⤚ ————

Should you wonder if I am indulging in that most reprehensible preacher's ploy of raising a straw man so as to knock him down with deft blows, let me give you an example of what I mean. A friend of mine, a godly man known for his faithfulness, on one occasion delivered a sermon of numbing irrelevance in my hearing. The occasion was a large Bible conference in Southern California that was convened for the deepening of the spiritual life. Given the state of affairs in that particular region at that particular time, it was a timely conference. But for some reason this godly, faithful preacher "felt led" to discuss in minute detail the problem raised by the Genesis account of the "sons of God" who were attracted to the "daughters of men." Most of the people there were not aware of this particular attraction and so were blissfully ignorant that there was any particular problem, for they had not spent time pondering whether the "sons of God" were actually angels or not. Accordingly, they had not delved into the issue of the sexuality of the angels (assuming that's who these beings were who knew pretty "daughters of men" when they saw them). The discourse not only took the allotted time but actually went overtime before we arrived at a conclusion as to the sons' identities and what it was they had been doing. (I regret to say I've forgotten what that conclusion was.) No one could accuse the old preacher of being pushed around by the interests of contemporary secular society. But neither would anyone have mistaken his message for one that would deepen the spiritual life of his listeners. Nor would it increase their effectiveness, living as they were in a secular society and showing more signs of being influenced by it than of having a lasting impact upon it.

The problem for the preacher who rightly aims at relevance is that the more the preaching moves in the direction of the hearers' interests, the greater is the danger of the preaching being irrelevant. It is the unique distinctiveness of the gospel that makes the difference in people's lives. But if the preaching has become so "relevant" that it differs little from the kind of discussion that fills the weary hours of talk shows, people may legitimately ask, "Why should we bother with this message called the gospel, which seems to be little more than a religious version of talk-show babble? Why go to the trouble of being religious, with all its attendant restrictions, if all I get in the end is the same kind of help for my problems that I can garner from other sources?" Good questions! On the other hand, such is the consumer mentality of today's culture that preachers who don't tackle the relevance issue may find great comfort in their own preaching, but it is doubtful if others will, because they will be found grazing elsewhere. This whole issue of relevance spells pressure for the preacher.

pressure of competition

When I was a kid growing up in the Brethren Assemblies in the north of England, I distinctly remember attending, against my will, an annual conference to which no specific preachers had been invited. The chairman would open the proceedings with prayer and then announce that any brother who "felt led of the Lord" should make his way to the platform to address the assembled multitude. Compared with the average-sized congregations these men were used to addressing, this was indeed a multitude. To my small mind, it was always perplexing how the Lord could be leading so many men to preach to us at the same time, for before the announcement was even concluded, the "led" men were on their way to

———————— ⪘⪘⪘⪙ ————————

Preachers who don't tackle the relevance issue may find great comfort in their own preaching, but it is doubtful if others will.

the platform in considerable numbers and with inconsiderate haste. On one occasion a number of them arrived at the narrow stair to the pulpit simultaneously and jammed there while the man on the other side made it to the desired position and they struggled to get free from the pack. The ones thus frustrated walked disconsolately back to their seats, where they waited to be "led" another day. This was my initial introduction to competition in ministry. But I have been no stranger to it ever since.

In addition, we have the not-so-subtle competition for influential pulpits, the outright competition for spectacular converts, the interdenominational competition for members, and the intradenominational competition over statistics. At pastors' conferences we often see the ill-disguised pride of the winners and the barely concealed pain of the losers. This competitive spirit pressures the preacher with such secularized force that the spiritual dynamics of faithfulness and powerfulness become distant memories.

So far we have noted that the preacher may well be pressured by societal and congregational factors to be less than faithful to the message and the ministry, with a resultant loss of life and power in preaching—a shortage of spiritual oxygen. There is one further area of pressure we must explore. It's very personal.

We have the not-so-subtle competition for influential pulpits, the outright competition for spectacular converts, the interdenominational competition for members, and the intradenominational competition over statistics.

chapter ❼

··

Dealing With Personal Pressure

Paul would probably have been labeled a Type A personality if he had lived in this day and age. He was certainly a hard driver, and there are plenty of indicators to suggest that he was consumed by burning intensity. In the old days they called it passion for souls. Nowadays people mutter darkly about workaholics. No doubt there were some people of passion in the old days who filled up some inadequacies in their lives by losing themselves in their work, and it is highly likely that there are some modern-day saints who, in their concern to avoid "toxic faith" and other ominous-sounding evangelical maladies, might have difficulty making the same team as the apostles. But what is the proper approach to ministry? When is enough enough?

I grew up in a culture (Britain) and a generation (post–World War II) in which Christians talked a lot about "stick-to-itiveness" and discipline and cost and sacrifice. I suppose this was natural, since we had just survived both a deep economic depression and a very nasty war. I distinctly remember one of the favorite Christian songs of the day: "Let me burn out for Thee, dear Lord, Let me burn out for Thee."

We were raised on stories about C. T. Studd, the intrepid missionary who took on China, India, and Africa, and who said things like this:

> Some people like to live within the sound of church or chapel bell.
>
> I'd rather run a rescue shop within a yard of hell.

When is enough enough?

And one of my favorite pieces of reading material was a little booklet Studd wrote called "The Chocolate Soldier," which suggested not very subtly that many Christians are superb soldiers until the heat is on and then they melt like—you guessed it—chocolate soldiers. The net result of this kind of an upbringing, coupled with a ministry that started out as part-time while I held down a responsible business position—and finished up more full-time than I had time for, was my commitment to hard-driving, nonstop Christian service. Once I brought this brand of Christianity across the ocean and across a few decades, I began to hear about workaholism and toxic faith and other new definitions of what I had been taught was normal Christianity. Very perplexing!

Bone idle or early grave?

So I went to talk to a dear friend, an experienced Southern Baptist pastor, and asked him about correct balance in the pastorate. His response was totally startling and, I subsequently discovered, most insightful. "Stuart," he said, "the pastorate is a position in which you can get away with either being bone idle or working yourself into an early grave."

It had never occurred to me that a pastor could be "bone idle." Admittedly I'd enjoyed the old joke that a minister was six days invisible and one day incomprehensible, but that was a joke. And I'd always been under the impression that I would be around as long as God wanted me around, so an early grave didn't make a lot of sense. So I asked him what he meant.

He replied that pastors can get away with not doing very much, if they are so inclined, because if they are answerable to anyone it is to a layperson. If the layperson asks awkward practical questions about the pastor's work, the pastor can give a high-sounding spiritual answer, and the layperson will probably leave him alone. But I was more interested in the other possibility. How did one work oneself to an early grave? He told me, in effect, that putting undue pressure on myself would do it in a hurry. But what is undue pressure?

I knew that my life, if it were governed by a sense of meeting the needs around me, would be one long tale of frustration, because of my inability to meet all the need, and exhaustion, because of the physical limits with which I had been endowed. On the other hand, I was aware that Paul had said, "But by the grace of God I am what I am, and his grace to me was not without effect. No, I worked harder than all of them—yet not I, but the grace of God that was with me" (1 Corinthians 15:10), and his word for "worked harder" literally meant to work to the point of exhaustion. So I knew being weary is not only permissible, it is probably necessary. I was also aware that Jesus himself took time out for the occasional dinner date and even suggested to his hyped disciples that they needed a break.

As I mulled these things over in my pastoral mind, I came across Paul's statement "I care very little if I am judged by you or by any human court; indeed, I do not even judge myself...Therefore judge nothing before the appointed time; wait till the Lord comes. He will bring to light what is hidden in darkness and will expose the motives of men's hearts. At that time each will receive his praise from God" (1 Corinthians 4:3, 5). It was the phrase "I do not even judge myself" that caught my attention; it sounded decidedly liberating. But it was also ominously open to abuse.

------------------ ⟞℘℘⟝ ------------------

"The pastorate is a position in which you can get away with either being bone idle or working yourself into an early grave."

The Need and the Call

Paul undoubtedly was painfully aware of human need on every hand. And his own temperament and sense of unique calling were highly motivating factors. So it would not be stretching things too much to imagine him tying himself in psychological knots as he endeavored to evaluate the effectiveness of his mission and the impact of his message. All the people who had not heard! All the great doors through which no one had ventured! All the confusion in the baby churches! All the epistles that needed to be written! All the issues that needed to be confronted! But apparently he had learned to live with the situation and, perhaps more surprisingly, to live with himself. "I do not even judge myself." Somehow he had managed to get himself out from under the intolerable load of personal pressure that many a high-minded, deeply devoted servant of God has labored beneath and sometimes sunk under. But let's face it: There are men and women of character today whose lives are dominated not only by congregational and societal pressures but also by personal pressure so intense that the joy has gone out of their lives and the power out of their pulpits.

Being weary is not only permissible,

it is probably necessary.

Enough Hours in the Day

A simple thought occurred to me one day. I had caught myself saying with the air of a martyr, "There aren't enough hours in the day." Having said it, I stopped to think about it. (I freely admit the reverse order: I do know it is advisable to think *before* speaking.) This is what I thought: "God knows what he wants me to accomplish. After all, I am his under-rower and his servant. If he knows what needs to be done and presumably knows how long it will take, it is reasonable for me to assume he will allot the right amount of time to accomplish his purposes." That being the case, I came to the astonishing conclusion that there is exactly the right number of hours in the day to accomplish what God wants to achieve. Not to believe this is to banish God to the ranks of the Egyptian taskmasters who demanded that the Israelites make bricks without straw. Ministry without enough time is the ecclesiastical equivalent of bricks without straw. The issue for me became not so much an intense, frustrated, never-ending attempt to meet every need on the horizon, but a sensible approach to filling the hours with the sort of responsible living that allowed me to be a person devoted to ministry rather than a machine driven by less noble motivations such as guilt, ambition, or even a diluted messianic complex. And responsible living clearly assumed an increased devotion to well-doing, but the well-doing certainly did not require the abandonment of such divinely ordained pleasures and delights as being a husband and a father and even, on occasion, an abysmal golfer.

But, you are probably saying to yourself or anyone within earshot, what has this to do with powerful, faithful, careful preaching? Quite a lot, actually, because effective preaching presupposes a spiritually healthy preacher, and that requires a preacher who handles the pressures of the calling well. We will explore in the next chapter specifically how Paul did it.

There is exactly the right number of hours in the day to accomplish what God wants to achieve.

chapter 8

Putting Things in Perspective

Phillips Brooks viewed preaching as "the best and happiest" thing to do. Now I think it would be true to say that as we have examined some of the pressures to which preachers are subjected, you could probably think of other words to describe your experience. Best and happiest? Hardly!

Let me remind you of the sense of privilege that seemed to pervade Paul's approach, even though he was perfectly forthright about the pressures of ministry. It is clear that he had figured out a way to handle the pressures so they did not diminish his sense of privilege, or to use Brooks' expression, his sense of doing the best and happiest thing in the world. The key word is *perspective.* He maintained the right kind of attitude toward both the upside of privilege and the downside of pressures because he had the balance of correct perspective. Without this no preacher can hope to stay fresh in the pulpit. If the ministry has become a burden, the messenger is in danger of becoming a bore. If the pressures have become intolerable, the preaching may become indigestible and the preacher insufferable. So let us look carefully at what Paul said about the perspective that he maintained:

> I care very little if I am judged by you or by any human court; indeed, I do not even judge myself…Therefore judge nothing before the appointed time; wait till the Lord comes. He will bring to light what is hidden in darkness and will expose the motives of men's hearts. At that time each will receive his praise from God (1 Corinthians 4:3, 5).

Discounting the pressure

Notice first that as far as congregational pressures were concerned, Paul's candid comment was "I care very little if I am judged by you." Of course, the same went for the societal pressures. This sounds like heady stuff! I can imagine an enthusiastic but misguided reader looking at what Paul said and deciding to call a special meeting of the elders, sitting them down, reading 1 Corinthians 4:3-5, then looking up over his horn-rimmed spectacles and saying, "On the authority of Scripture, and in the name of the Lord, phooey to you! I don't care two hoots what you think or say about my ministry. From now on, you can say and think what you like. I am a free man!" I don't doubt he would be more free than he had expected, to the point of being free to look for another pulpit. This is not the recommended approach. Neither is it an appropriate response to Paul's words.

Paul did not dismiss everything the Corinthians were saying, but he discounted most of it. He did not say that he did not care at all but rather that he cared "very little." There is a difference. Messed up as the Corinthians undoubtedly were, there was always the remote possibility that they had a point. Centuries later, Oliver Cromwell wrote to the Scottish Presbyterians, "I beseech thee in the bowels of Christ, consider that thou mightest be wrong." The same goes for all of us, the great apostle included.

There is little doubt that often the criticisms of a congregation are as ill-advised as they are ill-tempered. This means that while careful consideration must be given to what congregations say, even more care should be taken to evaluate their reasons for saying it. Only in this way can the validity of their statements be assessed. For example, it is not uncommon for pressures exerted in anger to have been birthed in an agenda. Reaction to the anger, often *in* anger, will therefore not only exacerbate the problem but will also never adequately identify the problem. Sometimes congregations are preoccupied, and these preoccupations become the basis for evaluation of the ministry. But preoccupations are the offspring of presuppositions, which may or may not be accurate. It is the task of the preacher to recognize the

While careful consideration must be given to what congregations say, even more care should be taken to evaluate their reasons for saying it.

—————— ⸙ ——————

preoccupations and to identify the presuppositions and then to evaluate them according to the preacher's mandate. Then and only then can the preacher determine if the congregational concerns are even remotely related to what it means for him to be an under-rower and steward. This will determine the validity of the criticism and how much concern is warranted.

Some time ago a friend of mine, a young father, came to me at the end of a sermon to tell me I should use shorter words. I asked him which words I had used that morning were, in his opinion, too long. He couldn't think of any. I told him I knew he was an exceptionally intelligent person and I was surprised he thought my vocabulary was too complicated. He replied that he was able to understand everything and it was not too complicated for him, but his young daughter had brought her friend to church that morning, and she had not understood everything. The presupposition in that case was that I should preach at such a level that a visiting ten-year-old could understand everything. His preoccupation was commendable and his presupposition understandable but questionable. I'll leave you to determine how much concern I needed to invest in his suggestion.

Let's Talk

When I embarked on my pastorate more than thirty-two years ago, I explained to the congregation that I was a total neophyte, having had neither training nor experience as a pastor. I reminded them that my only credentials were that I had discovered a wonderful book—the

Bible—and I possessed a willingness to explore it, a longing to explain it, and a desire to express it. I added, very genuinely, that if at any point members of the congregation felt I was out of order in what I preached or advocated in terms of application, they should not talk *about* me but rather come and talk *to* me. And I told them, "Bring your Bible!" This, incidentally, did two things. It cut down on the number of frivolous objections and raised the standard of debate and discussion to nobler heights than is often the case. It was possible on this basis to examine concerns and criticisms objectively in the light of Scripture rather than subjectively on less sure grounds. It became possible to discount many pressures rather quickly—not arbitrarily but on the basis of their having no biblical warrant. On the other hand, those concerns that clearly stemmed from Scripture were, on principle, taken seriously and dealt with accordingly. The result, quite frankly, was the glorious liberty of my being able to discount much that was ill-founded, ill-advised, ill-tempered, and ill-expressed—and to concentrate on that which was valid and significant.

I remember one member of the church being particularly incensed that I had, as she put it, dragged a lot of undesirable young people into the congregation. She came to me in the foyer of the church and said, "I haven't brought a Bible like you said, and I don't want you dragging the Bible into it. I just want you to know that you've no business preaching that we should be opening our congregation to the kind of people that we have worked hard to protect our own young people from." Frankly, while

---

If at any point members of the congregation felt I was out of order, I asked them not to talk about *me but rather to come and talk to* me. *And I told them, "Bring your Bible!"*

I was concerned that she was upset, I cared very little that I was judged by her on that particular point. She didn't have a biblical leg to stand on, and I was reasonably sure that I did. So as far as I was concerned, that was all that mattered. By the way, she got over it and is still a member.

Secularists can still be right even if they don't know the difference between an apostle and an epistle.

A similar approach can be taken in dealing with societal pressure because it will rarely be presented from a biblical perspective. It is necessary, of course, to recognize that secularists can still be right even if they don't know the difference between an apostle and an epistle. But when it comes to spiritual affairs, they are more likely to be wrong than right, and so their criticisms can be safely discounted. It is advisable to know what they are saying, why they are saying it, and where they are coming from in their arguments and their positions. It is even more beneficial if they can be shown why the preacher sees things from a completely different point of view. Obviously, if one comes from the position that the Bible is the final authority in matters of faith and practice, and the other sees the Bible as a collection of irrelevant but vaguely endearing stories that can be disregarded with impunity, there will be ample grounds for differing conclusions because there is no ground for common assumptions. The bottom line for the preacher is that he can discount much of what they say because they either do not understand what the Word says or they know perfectly well but consider it to be totally irrelevant.

Discontinuing the pressure

Paul's handling of personal pressures was somewhat different. He said, "I do not even judge myself." Now how does that fit into modern ideas of

Paul was neither casually complacent about his performance nor crippled by introspection.

———— ⟨⟨⟨⟩⟩⟩ ————

ministry based on job descriptions, goals, intermediate goals, measurable goals, semi-annual evaluations, and other business practices that have been baptized into church life? Did that mean that Paul was not account-able? Did he never have to sit down with the elders and have them check out his number of work hours per day, his visits per week, and his sick days per annum? Probably not, unless the elders were prepared to have their evaluation meetings in prison. But did he mean that he refused to be responsible or accountable? I think not. He talked often about believers being submissive to one another, and he insisted that the various members of the body were interrelated and did not have the freedom to decide that they could manage without one another. He was no loose cannon on the deck, but neither was he casually complacent about his performance or crippled by introspection. He stated insightfully, "My conscience is clear, but that does not make me innocent."

So he was aware of his conscience. He was no chloroformer of the conscience! He had apparently consulted it and found nothing that was obviously troublesome. But that did not prove anything more conclusive than that he did not have anything troubling his conscience. It certainly did not mean he was innocent of transgression. His conscience, like every other person's conscience, was capable of ignorance and bias and there-fore limited in its usefulness. It had its own special quirks and blind spots, its own peculiar dimensions of self-induced blindness, and it therefore was not a fit arbiter of his own effectiveness in ministry. This can easily be misunderstood. Someone might say, "Well, if my conscience is my guide but a faulty one, then it would be better to ignore it altogether." That would be drawing a false conclusion from Paul's statement.

evaluating Motives

Paul does not advocate ignoring the conscience, but he says there is something much more significant when it comes to the evaluation of ministry (or of life itself), and that is the knowledge that the Lord is the only one capable of accurate evaluation. God alone can search the intricacies of the heart and unravel the tangled web of motives, aspirations, self-delusions, and assorted aberrations. To realize that the ultimate evaluation of ministry, which will be conducted by the Lord himself, is what really matters and to know that it is not based on purely external criteria, is indeed sobering. Then to recognize that the Lord is concerned not only about *what* is done but *why* it is done is to come to grips with ministry at a deep and realistic level. He will examine the motives of our hearts and bring to light the hidden things, and then he will make his evaluation.

Shortly after I resigned my business career, I had difficulty adjusting to the realities of full-time ministry as opposed to those of the business world. I was not behaving very well, and to compound matters I developed a serious throat infection that refused to respond to treatment. I was told by my doctor not only to stop preaching but also to stop talking. He reinforced his instructions with a solemn "If you don't do what I'm telling you, your preaching days may be over." He was probably trying to scare me into subjection, and he succeeded.

I spent a miserable few weeks second-guessing my decision to leave banking to concentrate on ministry. One day I had a searing, troubling

---

To recognize that the Lord is concerned
not only about what *is done but* why *it*
is done is to come to grips with ministry
at a deep and realistic level.

thought. I wondered if I would ever be content if I could never preach again. The thought persisted and eventually became framed in a question that seemed to come from the Lord himself: "Stuart Briscoe, what do you love most—preaching *about* me, or *me*?" It was a question I had trouble addressing, because I knew it would expose the motives behind my preaching, and I didn't like what I was discovering about myself. There was a certain excitement about preaching, a sense of being able to do something and do it reasonably well. It was thrilling to be in demand. It was gratifying to have people actually sit down and listen to me. It was enough to turn any young man's head, and I'm afraid it turned mine.

"What do you love most about God— preaching about him, or him?"

I'm thankful I learned a big lesson early. A preacher's motives matter more than a preacher's methods. If what is going on in a preacher's heart is not right, what is coming out of his mouth will be all wrong. To accept this is to agree that maintaining a proper relationship with the Lord is crucial. Preaching shipwrecks all too easily take place when this basic truth is forgotten or ignored. The pressurized winds from many quarters soon drive a preacher off course if the preacher does not keep a weather eye on spiritual bearings.

But what does this mean in practical terms? Perhaps the Lord's encounter with Peter after the traumatic days of the first Easter gives us a necessary clue. You remember the incident:

> When they had finished eating, Jesus said to Simon Peter, "Simon son of John, do you truly love me more than these?" "Yes, Lord," he said, "you know that I love you." Jesus said, "Feed my lambs." Again Jesus said, "Simon son of John, do

you truly love me?" He answered, "Yes, Lord, you know that I love you." Jesus said, "Take care of my sheep." The third time he said to him, "Simon son of John, do you love me?" Peter was hurt because Jesus asked him the third time, "Do you love me?" He said, "Lord, you know all things; you know that I love you." Jesus said, "Feed my sheep" (John 21:15-17).

Apparently there was a clear connection between loving the Lord and feeding lambs and feeding sheep and taking care of sheep. And there still is. For preachers this means that the freshness of their experience of the Lord's grace is so powerful that their hearts are full of love for the Lord, and out of a well of gratitude their service flows. This means preachers' hearts are filled with appreciation, not only for initial grace that led to reconciliation and regeneration but also for continuous grace that leaves them in a constant state of loving gratitude and genuine, unforced appreciation. Thus preaching becomes the overflow of a full heart. Should the heart not overflow because the inflow of grace has ceased, either through outright blockages or downright neglect, then the flow becomes a trickle, and the trickle leads inevitably to a desert in which parched souls find little refreshment.

A preacher's motives matter more than a preacher's methods.

Beware of Blockages

The outright blockages are related to the kind of sins to which preachers are particularly susceptible. Pride is an obvious one, because preachers think they know more than the people they are teaching. That may be true; in fact, one could reasonably hope it is true. But it is only true because they have been gifted by God for reasons known only to him and afforded the opportunity to study and to prepare

Preaching becomes the overflow of a full heart.

———— <small>⌒∿∿∿⌒</small> ————

because of the faithfulness and support of the people they are tempted to regard as inferior. A.W. Tozer, the well-known Christian and Missionary Alliance preacher, who left school at age fourteen, once told my friend Keith Price, a Canadian preacher, "We have an advantage over the graduates because we know that we don't know." No pride there, despite the fact that at the time he was one of the most sought-after preachers in America. It seems to me that whatever the depth of our knowledge of Scripture, we must never lose sight of the fact that there are mysteries which we will never plumb, and the things we know we know only because they have been revealed. If we know anything, it is because God in his mercy opened our blind eyes. A constant reminder of these simple truths should thwart the tendency toward pride, a particularly obvious Achilles' heel of the preacher.

Then there is the temptation to become so used to telling other people what to do about what God says that the preacher overlooks the need to do it himself. Surely the most effective sermon is the one that has gripped the heart of the preacher because the powerful Word has first ministered to him or her. This means that the approach to Scripture must be much more than a frantic search for texts or a professional selection of topics. It requires the preacher to commune with the Lord in private and apply the Word in person. Bishop Taylor Smith, a British preacher, had an unusual habit of walking up to people and asking them, "And what has the Lord shown you today?" Some people found it most disconcerting, mainly those who had not taken the time to give God a chance to say anything to them. But the question was not at all disconcerting to those whose well was full and ready to overflow. Their response would probably have been, "Bishop, I'm glad you asked. How much time do you have?"

Breakdown in Discipline

The neglect comes from a failure in discipline. I do not just refer to the more obvious breakdowns in discipline that have resulted in preachers being led away into sexual sin and disgrace, although this is clearly a cause for monumental concern. I am thinking more of the gradual neglect of the Word and prayer, the failure to nourish the preacher's own soul, occasioned often by the pressures of which we have been speaking. The preacher must maintain a priority of reading, studying, meditating, and praying based on the Word and supplemented by the kind of materials most likely to lead to a close walk with the Lord, a walk characterized by obedience to the Lord and dependence on the Spirit, a walk that commends itself to the watching world and is itself a living illustration of the Word preached. A preacher must not fall into an attitude that tacitly tells the people, "Do what I say, not what I do." Paul knew better than that. When he wrote to young Timothy, he was able to say, "You, however, know all about my teaching, my way of life, my purpose, faith, patience, love, endurance, persecutions, sufferings" (2 Timothy 3:10-11).

Paul unashamedly pointed to his own life as a reasonable expression of what he taught. He insisted, "Not that I have already...been made perfect," but it was obvious to anybody who chose to look that his determined intention was to "press on to take hold of that for which Christ Jesus took hold of me" (Philippians 3:12). So Paul avoided the trap of suggesting that he was a model of perfection to be emulated, but he was comfortable pointing out that he and other preachers can realistically be expected to preach by word and by way of life.

If we know anything, it is because God

in his mercy opened our blind eyes.

If I was ever in any doubt about the necessity to care for my own spiritual life and relationship with the Lord, the doubts have long since been banished by many of the young adults in the church I serve. Repeatedly they come to my wife or me and say, "We want to thank you for being faithful. We look to you, you know. We come from dysfunctional families, and we have never had role models. We are new Christians, and we don't know what we are supposed to do, so we listen to your teaching, but we also watch the way you do things. We hope you don't mind." We don't, of course, but we hurriedly remind them that while we have a calling to fulfill that requires faithfulness, we, of all people, are conscious of our own feet of clay and the need to keep our inner lives in close touch and harmony with the Lord. And we ask these dear young people to pray for us as we pray for and minister to them.

So how do we ensure that our preaching is powerful and vital? By reminding ourselves that preaching is a glorious privilege with its own peculiar pressures that we need to overcome by maintaining a correct perspective through living before the Lord faithfully. We must remember that the ultimate evaluation belongs to God and, therefore, our main job is to prepare ourselves before the Lord so that we might present our sermons before the people.

We, of all people, are conscious of our own feet of clay and the need to keep our inner lives in close touch and harmony with the Lord.

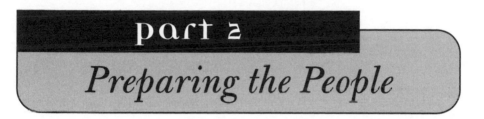

part 2
Preparing the People

chapter 9

"The View From the Pew"

The story is told of an old British minister who once announced, "The offertory will now be taken. This week it will be devoted entirely to the extermination of dry rot in the pulpit and worms in the pews." I have no way of knowing if the muffled giggles with which this announcement was greeted adversely affected the offertory. But apparently the congregation saw some similarities between his preaching and "dry rot" and accordingly had spent many a weary hour squirming like "worms in the pews." (In case the humor of the statement did not cross the Atlantic, let me say that in British English *dry* means "boring" and *rot* means "nonsense," so the unintentional double-entendre was magnificent.)

It should never be so! But let's face it: The mechanics of the pulpit play a major role in the formation of attitudes in the pew. Dry rot in pulpits and worms in pews are not unrelated. It is clear, however, that much can be done by those who lead a worship service to ensure that participants are interested, involved, intrigued, and inspired. In other words, much can be done to make both the preaching more palatable and the listening more enjoyable. Charles Haddon Spurgeon's delightful dictum was "Pleasantly profitable let all our sermons be"—to which we may add, "Pleasantly profitable let the context in which the preaching takes place be."

A pleasant place for preaching

Most pastoral preaching takes place in the context of a worship service. The significance and role of preaching in the worship service

Preaching must remain a pre-eminent and indispensable part of worship.

---

varies considerably from one tradition to another. I regard the exposition of Scripture as a vitally important part of the worship experience, and I believe it should play a significant role in focusing the attention of worshippers on the Lord so they will hear his voice, know his will, and perform his bidding—all of which are part and parcel of worship. Keeping Archbishop William Temple's superb definition of worship in mind has helped me greatly:

> Worship is the submission of all our nature to God. It is the quickening of conscience by His holiness; the nourishment of mind with His truth; the purifying of imagination by His beauty; the opening of the heart to His love; the surrender of will to His purpose—and all of this gathered up in adoration, the most selfless emotion of which our nature is capable and therefore the chief remedy for that self-centeredness which is our original sin and the source of all actual sin.[1]

There is no doubt that the conscience, mind, imagination, heart, and will of which he spoke can be addressed in a variety of ways, but I believe the preaching of the Word is a pre-eminent and indispensable way of doing this. Therefore, preaching must remain a pre-eminent and indispensable part of worship.

Having said this, however, I have to admit that for a long time my unspoken and unconscious attitude to worship services was that they consisted of preliminaries that should be dispatched as soon as possible before the real action—the preaching—took place. This was brought home to me rather forcefully one day when I talked to some of our most sincere people in the church. They habitually arrived late—not just late but really late, and mysteriously the same amount of time late each week.

In other words, their starting time for the 10:30 service was 10:55. On the button! In response to my inquiry, they told me, quite frankly, "Oh, we're not interested in the preliminaries. We just come for the preaching." I realized that they had picked up this attitude from those of us who were responsible for leading the people in worship. In their minds preliminaries were irrelevant and preaching was significant. It did not require great observational powers to see how they had gained this impression. Anyone attending the church could see immediately that the preaching received a lot of attention. For example, everybody was given upon arrival a detailed outline of the sermon, which obviously had not grown on a tree. They could see in a moment that a considerable amount of time and care had been invested in it. But the rest of the service was, by comparison, thrown together. It was not unusual for the leaders to select hymns on the way in to the service, and on one occasion when we forgot to do even that, we covered by asking the congregation for "favorites."

This, of course, would not happen in a liturgical service where a structure is in place—in some instances so firmly in place that preaching is relegated to a homily of minute proportions. And for totally different reasons, the same thing can happen in services where *worship* is a synonym for the repetitive singing of contemporary songs and the sharing of personal experiences, which activities take up the bulk of the allotted time.

I came to see that the issue I needed to address was the relationship of preaching—an integral part of the worship service—with the other integral aspects of the service. My tendency had been to concentrate on the nourishment of mind and the surrender of will—to use the archbishop's phrases—at the expense of, as he put it, the quickening of conscience, the purifying of imagination, and the opening of the heart. I suspected that other worship leaders perhaps had similar problems of imbalance stemming from emphases at different points of the spectrum. So I decided to take some action.

predictable worship

Dr. Howie Stephenson, when he was worship leader at Fullerton Evangelical Free Church, told me on one occasion, "Predictability

"Predictability breeds boredom."

———— ⟡ ————

breeds boredom." It occurred to me that the preacher who inherits a congregation of bored squirmers when the time for preaching finally arrives has done himself a disservice and has hardly encouraged the people to be ready and eager for the Word. On the other hand, if the service has been filled with ingredients that have motivated the people, they will be much more likely to listen eagerly and attentively. A brief review of our church's normal worship service revealed a major element of predictability.

I had grown up in a Brethren Assembly where the morning service was always a Communion service called the breaking of bread. It was believed that the Holy Spirit should be free to lead the congregation through any of the people present, a concept based loosely on 1 Corinthians 14:26-40. Even in such a situation, which was the ultimate in "unstructured" (there was nothing organized, except that the elements of Communion must be administered before noon), there was a relentless predictability about the service. It was ironic that the proponents of this type of worship criticized the Anglicans for what they characterized unfairly as "vain repetitions" without apparently recognizing that they were in danger of being pots who call kettles black. There was enough predictability to go around.

The other side of the coin also had to be considered. If predictability breeds boredom, what does unpredictability produce? Discomfort. So now we have a real conundrum. If predictability breeds boredom, and unpredictability breeds discomfort, what should be done? I came to the conclusion that we should have only predictable elements in the service, but they should be presented in ways that are not always predictable. It seemed to me that this way we could possibly have our cake and eat it too. So with some friends and colleagues, I formed a worship-preparation group to plan services that would be predictably unpredictable. We were not interested in novelty for the sake of novelty, nor did we commit ourselves to entertaining people who had little or no concept of worship. We were determined to see, inasmuch as we were able, that the worship experience would leave God revered and people renewed.

The first thing we had to do was agree on the predictable elements of a worship experience. Naturally we turned to the Scriptures for help. Our presupposition was that anything for which there is a biblical rationale should be classified as a predictable worship service element. We developed the following list. (It was not intended to be exhaustive, and some elements were more obvious than others. There was no particular relevance to the order of the elements. If my memory serves me correctly, we just listed them as they came to mind.)

1. Call to worship
2. Prayer
3. Testimony
4. Ministry reports
5. Music
6. Announcements
7. Scripture reading
8. Drama
9. Preaching
10. Offerings
11. Commissioning
12. Sacraments/ordinances
13. Benediction

If predictability breeds boredom,
what does unpredictability produce?

I think that most of these elements would be acceptable to most people without question. Some might have doubts about drama, for example, but we had carefully noted the dramatic methodology of some of the prophets and the graphic ways in which the Lord used incidents to illustrate the points he was making. David Watson wrote:

> The Bible, too, is full of *drama*, as seen once again in the great feasts. Some of the prophets, such as Ezekiel and Agabus, communicated their message in highly dramatic form, which no doubt made a much more vivid impression on the onlookers than bare words. Jesus himself was the supreme master of communication, and there is little doubt that some of his teaching and parables had considerable dramatic and visual content as well as matchless words.[2]

predictably unpredictable

We then set about thinking of the different (unpredictable) ways that these predictable elements could be incorporated into the service. Remember, the point was not novelty. We were interested in helping to revitalize our services. It was not too difficult, once we set our minds to it, to realize that there are many ways of doing the same things. For example, they can be done

- by different people,
- at different times,
- from different places, and
- in different fashions.

To put it another way, in many worship services one can easily predict before entering the sanctuary *who* will do *what,* from *where, when*, and *how!*

call to worship

For example, one can reasonably assume that the minister (who) will begin (when) with a call to worship (what) from the lectern (where). Granted, it is probably not advisable to conclude a service with a call to worship. (Maybe a wake-up call would be more appropriate at times!) There is not a lot of room for unpredictability as to when the call to worship occurs. But having said that, why does the minister have to do it? Why does it have to be spoken? And why does it have to be done from the front of the church? We decided that sometimes our trumpeters (who) would bring a fanfare (what) as the call to worship from the rear of the balcony (where). That gets people's attention! Another time it could be a couple of children (who) standing up in the pews (where) and saying, "We're glad we're here, and we're glad you're here, so now that we are here, let's worship" (what). Then the more predictable approach of a choir (who) singing an introit (what) from the aisles (where) instead of from the choir loft would still have a dash of unpredictability about it. All these things would make the occasion when the minister actually issues the call to worship from the lectern seem like a refreshing change. In fact, an approach of this kind would mean that a whole month would go by without repetition of something as predictable as the call to worship. And it is just possible that people may be so intrigued by this previously totally predictable part of the service that they would make a special effort to be there at the start, which is in itself a great reason for trying it.

predictable prayer?

But what about prayer? The easiest, and therefore the most common, way of doing it is to have the minister do it. It usually comes at a predictable time, and because it is done by the same person, it often has predictable content and is led from a predictable place. So why not ring in some changes? In some churches, for instance, the Lord's Prayer is always used, and in others it is never used. In some the collects and creeds (which I recognize are affirmations rather than prayers) are always recited, while in others they are not even known. So where there is liturgical predictability, it is easy to see where some variation could take place by a relaxation of some approaches and the incorporation of others. Conversely, where there is liturgical ignorance or even resistance, a judicious incorporation of some of the church's historical gems could be most edifying and gratifying.

What about inviting a family to lead the congregation in prayer?

———————— ❦ ————————

Perhaps this is a little too radical for some. So what about inviting a family to lead the congregation in prayer? Dad could lead off with the praise and thanksgiving; Mom could follow with expressions of repentance and contrition (or maybe the reversal of roles would be considered by some to be more appropriate); teenage Jimmy could ask the Lord for his blessing on missionaries whom Jimmy knows personally because he visited them in the field last summer; his sister Jeanie could follow with petitions for some of the sick and elderly, including the old people she had visited in a retirement home earlier in the week; while Junior could bring up the rear with a suitable conclusion. We did this on one occasion with a family who had a child with Down syndrome. He had no intention of being left out, and neither did we intend to leave him out, but nobody was ready for his loud and clear "For Jesus' sake, amen" with which the prayer time ended. That is the only occasion I remember a prayer time ending in surprised, delighted laughter mingled with tears.

There is much debate about congregational participation. "Unchurched Harry," who has been immortalized by my friend Bill Hybels of Willow Creek Community Church, does not want to be involved, so some services are crafted so he won't be—for the time being, at any rate. Other people feel that *nonparticipatory worship* is an oxymoron on the order of *jumbo shrimp*. Accordingly, we have debated whether to have a prayer time in which the people in the pews do the praying. This is not a problem if the congregation is made up of saints (that congregation has other problems), but it can be difficult if visitors, who are not used to church, are put in embarrassing positions. On occasion we have someone stand up and say, "Now we're going to pray. Some of you do it regularly. Others may not have done it for a while. So we'll help you. Everybody stand up, please, and form a group of four people. Now tell them your name and which color best represents how you feel today." After a couple of minutes, the leader says, "Now that we're a little more comfortable" (the buzz of conversation mingled with laughter will indicate this to be the case), "we're going to do some 'please, God' prayers no longer than one sentence each. Each sentence will begin with 'Please, God…' and you'll finish it in your own words. Everybody can do that. Now remember, no more than one sentence." After a few moments of participation, the leader says, "Maybe some of you have some 'sorry' prayers. Don't worry; you don't have to say them out loud, but this is a good time to pray them quietly." After a minute's silence (which will seem like a long time), the leader says, "Now it's time for 'thank you' prayers. Often we say 'please' but forget to say 'Thank you.' So this is our chance. Go around the group, and each one pray a prayer starting with 'Thank you, God, for…' "

Now I admit that this could be embarrassing to a few people, but if it is led in a friendly, easy manner, the embarrassment will be minimized and the advantages will be maximized. One lady told me, "I brought my husband to church for the first time today, and my heart stopped beating when your wife got up to do one of her 'pew-prayer times.' Each person in the group prayed, and then there was silence for a moment before I heard my husband's voice praying—the first time I'd ever heard that in our marriage. He prayed, 'Thank you, God, that I finally made it here. Amen.' Later on he prayed, 'Please, God, help me to figure out what this is all about. Amen.' I believe the Lord heard his prayers. And I know the other couple in the group did, because they said to me as we left, 'We'll be praying for your husband.' "

Testimonies

Testimonies are not a substitute for preaching, but they can and should be exciting illustrations of what the One of whom the preacher preaches does in people's lives. Many people sitting in pews will settle down to a sermon with a certain air of resignation. They may not articulate it, but their attitude is "Well, here we go; the preacher will now do what he's paid to do and tell us what we're supposed to know." But if a colleague or friend stands up to speak, that's a different matter. Immediately they'll be intrigued:

Identify a person who has a story to tell that specifically illustrates the point you will be trying to make in the sermon.

———————— ◦◦◦ ————————

"What's he going to say? Why is he up there? What does he know about public speaking? Wild horses wouldn't get me up there!" Testimonies certainly have their place in a worship experience, but care should be taken to identify that place and stick to it. Testimonies done badly, incessantly, regularly, repetitively, and trivially can have a devastating effect, but done well, appropriately, occasionally, and relevantly can pack a powerful punch. We have used testimonies in a variety of ways and at different times.

On special occasions such as Thanksgiving or at the end of a series of messages on a certain topic, we sometimes have a "roving mike," when staff members move around the congregation, responding to various people as they indicate that they have something to say. It's important that someone is in charge of this exercise so things don't get out of hand. (Some people are frustrated preachers waiting for their chance to have an audience. Others have an ax to grind, a project to promote, an exhortation to present, or simply a desire to hear their own voices.) So the leader must spell out the purpose and direction of the time of testimony in terms general enough so as not to hinder what the Spirit may want to say, but specific enough to keep people on track. To do this we have a golden rule: The ones holding the roving mikes must not let go of them, or they may never get them back!

A more helpful approach has been for us to identify a person who has a story to tell that specifically illustrates the point the preacher will be trying to make in the sermon. This person is asked if he or she would be willing to speak about the particular topic. Those who agree are asked to write what they want to say. There are two reasons for this. The first is the time factor. We know how much time we want to invest in the testimony, and we also know that people can easily lose track of time. The second reason is that people often need help formulating and expressing their thoughts. Once the testimony has been written, a worship leader spends time with the testifier, and the presentation is finalized. I know of few things more powerful and intriguing in a worship service than a carefully chosen, prepared, and presented illustration by someone speaking from personal experience.

Another method we've utilized on occasion is the interview of a number of persons who have something to say about a certain topic. For example, on one occasion I preached on violence, and one of my colleagues interviewed a policeman, a public defender, a judge, and a teenager, all of whom had experience on the subject but from widely diverse points of view. They were all Christians and members of the church. The things they had to say were of great interest because they not only described the real issues in living color, but they also demonstrated that Christians may have differing perspectives on the same subject. This illustrated the fact that simplistic answers are not appropriate responses to complex problems.

MUSIC, MUSIC, MUSIC

There are more opportunities for unpredictable predictability in music than in any other area. The old line that when the devil was thrown out of heaven he landed in the choir loft was probably originated by a frazzled preacher and has been perpetuated by his equally frazzled successors. What preacher has not found music to be a minefield? But how many have discovered how to turn a minefield into a gold mine? I would number myself in that fortunate brotherhood, because of the excellent colleagues who work with me in that area. But this does not mean that all is clear sailing in the musical aspect of our worship services, particularly because we insist on a measure of unpredictability.

When a church is made up of a specific homogeneous group of people, it should not be too difficult to keep them musically happy, because there will probably be a homogeneity to their musical tastes as well as to everything else. But if a church has committed itself to attracting a diverse group of people because it wants to demonstrate its call to be something the world knows little about—unity in diversity—then music probably will be a hot potato. At the same time, there are

What preacher has not found
music to be a minefield?

few tools more readily available to us in the worship experience that can keep people alert, intrigued, and involved.

If to the question of who does what where and when is added the question of how, and all are applied to music, it's easy to see how the predictable element of music can be presented in many unpredictable ways, or in other words, how people can be delivered from boredom while being saved from discomfort. I realize, of course, that churches are limited by the amount and variety of the musical resources available to them. But there's no reason they shouldn't utilize the resources they do have as creatively as possible.

One of the hurdles is called *suitable worship music.* Many a preacher has stumbled over this one, and many more have skinned their shins. There are in the church those who are convinced God stopped inspiring church musicians when Charles Wesley died, while others are equally convinced he only discovered worship music when Keith Green was born. In my humble opinion, both positions betray a certain arrogance. These people often seem to equate worshipful music with personal taste. And there is nothing quite so formidable as taste when it comes to church music.

It must be admitted that taste is a learned behavior. If I invited you over to my house for dinner and offered you snails, you would probably be upset—unless, of course, you had developed your culinary tastes in France. And if I went to a friend's house in certain parts of my native north of England, I would not be at all put off by being served tripe and onions. But most Americans would, only because they haven't acquired the taste—or the stomach—for such delicacies. But I promise you, if they stayed around long enough and tried hard enough, they could learn to enjoy them. So it is with musical tastes. Of course, sometimes we run into problems when people with strongly developed tastes—or distastes—find a theological rationale for their preferences or prejudices. Then care has to be taken to unravel the taste from the text, or separate the malady from the melody.

All churches can intersperse traditional hymns with contemporary songs. The former may be more theological (and incomprehensible), the latter more experiential (and trivial), but together they can often balance each other out. Some enterprising soul may want to fit the words of an old hymn to a well-known modern tune, bearing in mind that this is exactly what such ecclesiastical luminaries as William Booth and Martin Luther dared to do. Or you may find someone in the congregation with a way with words who could write some lyrics to be sung to a traditional tune. This would not be too far removed from what that stern old reformer John Calvin did in Geneva when he authorized the psalms to be sung to specially composed tunes which were known by his deriders as "Geneva jingles."

Should the church's resources permit, there is no limit to the kinds of music that can enhance the worship experience. Some people love choirs singing anthems; others prefer groups singing country. For some the organ should be used on Sunday morning and not drums, but on Sunday evening drums are appropriate and not the organ. Why? I've no idea! But it's probably for the same reason that in my childhood assembly there were no instruments on Sunday morning but there was an organ on Sunday evening. I never did discover the reason.

In our church we run the gamut from cantatas to bluegrass, from Bach to Bill Gaither, from brass quintets to jazz ensembles, from organ to bassoon, from soloists to quartets. Not everybody appreciates everything (including me), but nobody appreciates nothing, or more positively, everybody appreciates something. And nobody goes to sleep. So when I

———— 〰 ————

Care has to be taken to separate

the malady from the melody.

get up to preach, people do tend to be on the front edge of their seats instead of slumping in their pews. That is, of course, assuming we have the music first and the sermon last. But that's a little too predictable, so sometimes we reverse the order to see if anyone is paying attention.

There is no need for me to take you through our list of predictables and describe all our unpredictable ways of doing things. If you have never done so, why not make a list of acceptable predictables, then think of four or five ways of doing each? Then keep bringing on changes, but explain to the people what you are doing. And keep track of what you've done, because you'll soon find it's all too easy to slip back into doing things the old way because it was the easy way. This way takes time and work, but we're talking about leading people in worship, so there can be no more important or worthwhile work, can there? Perhaps these thoughts will stir your creative juices, which in turn could lead to new ways of leading worship that is rich and meaningful.

Naturally it is helpful if the service can be crafted in such a way that there is discernible cohesion among the various elements. But it should not be assumed that people will necessarily notice the train of thought as readily as the ones who have worked for a number of hours during the week—or probably over a number of weeks—in preparation. It may be very helpful if the worship leader gently steers people through the various elements and briefly identifies for them the ways these elements enhance one another.

Endnotes

1. William Temple, *Readings in St. John's Gospel* (London: MacMillan, 1947), 68.

2. David Watson, *I Believe In the Church* (London: Hodder and Stoughton, 1978), 325.

There is no limit to the kinds of music that can enhance the worship experience.

part 3
Preparing the Message

chapter ❿

Developing a Preaching Plan

Dan Baumann wrote in the *Leadership Handbooks of Practical Theology:*

> Quality preaching does not happen by accident. It is the
> result of hard work, creative thinking, careful research, and a
> dependence upon the Holy Spirit. In other words, there is no
> shortcut to homiletical excellence.[1]

This will not surprise many preachers, but I suspect that some
people in the pews may not have suspected that preaching requires
such things as "hard work, creative thinking, and careful research."
They more likely think as did the preacher's son who listened to his
friends talk about what they wanted to be when they grew up. Each
wanted to emulate his father. The artist's son said all his dad did was
splash some paint on a canvas and people paid a hundred dollars for
it, so he was going to be a painter. The writer's son said his dad put a
few words on paper and he was paid a salary for it, so writing was the
way for him to go. The preacher's son, not to be left out, said he was
going to be a preacher because all his dad did was talk for ten minutes
a week and it took twelve men to carry in the cash. There's a lot more
to preaching than talking for ten minutes and waiting for the cash to
come rolling in.

The athlete who gives the impression that he is playing the game
effortlessly does so because of long hours in training before he steps
into the public arena. The businessman who makes a smooth, flawless

A sermon is the product of a lifetime rather than the product of a specific amount of time.

———— ❧ ————

presentation does so only because of the time he has spent marshaling his facts and polishing his delivery. So it is with the preacher. Some preachers actually claim to spend one hour in preparation for every minute they speak. This is a claim I've never made because I've never kept track, and there is a sense in which a sermon is the product of a lifetime rather than the product of a specific amount of time. Nevertheless, the point is that considerable hard work must take place behind the scenes before the preacher stands before the people.

In his 1911 Yale lectures, J.H. Jowett quoted the English judge Lord Bowen, who said, "Cases are won in chambers." Jowett explained:

> If a barrister is to practically conquer his jury before he meets them, by the victorious strength and sway of his preparation, shall it be otherwise with a preacher, before he seeks the verdict of his congregation? With us too, cases are won in chambers! Men are not deeply influenced by extemporized thought. They are not carried along by a current of fluency which is ignorant where it is going. Mere talkativeness will not put people in bonds. Happy-go-lucky sermons will lay no necessity upon the reason nor put any strong constraint upon the heart. Preaching that costs nothing accomplishes nothing. If the study is a lounge, the pulpit will be an impertinence.[2]

"Hard work" is all too descriptive of the situation facing preachers when they get around to sermon preparation. Many of them find preparation so difficult that they put it off as long as they can, filling their time with all kinds of activities to delay the moment when they must sit down to stare once more at a blank sheet of paper that dares them to fill it with pearls of wisdom. Other preachers are so busy dealing with genuine and necessary pastoral concerns that the time for study is pushed further and further toward the back burner until Saturday night arrives and there's nothing cooking. To approach sermon preparation tired and weary at the end of a week is to invite problems that will not hesitate to accept the invitation.

But there are ways to make the task of sermon preparation a delight rather than drudgery. It's possible to open the windows and let some fresh air into the study, but this does not mean preparation will not require work. It simply means that the work should be pleasurable and, accordingly, will stand a much better chance of being profitable.

planned preaching

One of the obvious ways to avoid this kind of pressure is to know before Saturday night what you're going to preach on before Sunday morning. I believe planning has marked advantages, but not everybody agrees. No less a preacher than Spurgeon not only eschewed a preaching plan but also advised his students against it. He felt that for preaching to be relevant, it was necessary for the preacher to be responsive to what was happening in the world. His point was that if you had planned what you were going to say before you knew what was going to happen, how could you be up-to-date when it happened? Good point! But, with all due respect to the "prince of preachers," there are very few preachers who can study as quickly and as effectively (and remember what they've studied) as Spurgeon. He had twelve thousand volumes in his personal library, and for his book *Commenting and Commentaries* he personally reviewed no fewer than "some three or four thousand" of them[3] and had a working knowledge of what the rest had to say. Not everyone has the mental capacity of a

———— ❧ ————

There are ways to make the task of sermon preparation a delight rather than drudgery.

Spurgeon; neither are there so many monumental events occurring as to require specific sermons to address them. If something really significant happens unexpectedly, there's no reason a planned series should not be interrupted. Or a reference to the event worked into an already planned message could be all that is necessary.

What, then, are the advantages of planning? First, there are definite advantages for the preacher. Once the course is set for a period of preaching, it is easier to gather material. The preacher can enlist members of the congregation to look out for information related to the subject. In the course of a busy day, the preacher can utilize spare moments that otherwise might slip away. For instance, the preacher may listen to tapes related to the subject while driving between hospitals on routine visits. Resource materials can either be purchased or borrowed in advance. All these things are stored in the preacher's mind, allowing time for the kind of thoughtful processing of information that the sermon needs if it is to have depth.

There are marked advantages also for the congregation. Once members of the congregation know in advance what the preacher will address, they can read the relevant Scriptures and come prepared to hear the Word with an enhanced sense of anticipation and understanding. Some might even wish to study in advance and then listen to the preacher. One group of young businessmen in my congregation does this and then listens to me, as they told me, to see if I get it right. And, of course, if people are actively involved in bringing friends and neighbors to share in the worship experience, they'll be able to identify topics that may be of particular interest and help to specific people so they can make plans to invite them.

Those responsible for the worship service will also find it advantageous to know in advance what to expect from the sermon. This helps them to plan the kind of service ingredients of which we spoke in the last chapter.

What kind of planning is advisable? Some preachers have the privilege of a study leave in which they devote themselves to prayer, study, and reflection for a week or two with the express purpose of planning a

I've given each member of the congregation

a piece of paper on which was written,

"I would like to hear a sermon, no longer

than _____ minutes, on the subject

'What the Bible says about _____.' "

year's preaching. They then emerge from this experience refreshed, focused, and ready to go. I must admit that I have never done this. Not, I hasten to add, because the church in which I minister did not grant the leave, but because I never asked. I have limited myself to planning one series at a time, but of course there is nothing sacred about either method.

Preachers who minister in a more liturgical setting will often utilize the lectionary as a basis for their planning. In this method the preacher follows the events of the Christian year and thus ensures that in a year's preaching, the salient aspects of biblical truth are covered. A possible disadvantage is that the preacher who stays a number of years in the same church may run out of things to say if the same texts keep reappearing.

The choice of subject is a good place to begin. I'm often asked, "How do you choose what to preach about?" The answer is that a number of factors go into the decision. I often get suggestions from the congregation. Sometimes I ask them to communicate to me what type of messages they would like to hear. For instance, on more than one occasion I've given each member of the congregation a piece of paper on which was written, "I would like to hear a sermon, no longer than _____ minutes, on the subject 'What the Bible says about _____.' "

What is burning in my heart that
needs to see the light of day?

———————— ❧ ————————

The responses have been illuminating. I noticed that a number of people were more concerned about the duration of the sermon than the content. Others missed the point with suggestions such as "What the Bible says about Martin Luther." One bright spark took the opportunity to pull my leg, suggesting I preach a sermon no longer than ten minutes on "What the Bible says about God." But literally hundreds have responded seriously and have given many great ideas for sermon series. Even when the congregation is not formally asked to suggest subjects, I often ask individuals informally or they've volunteered suggestions to me. The pastoral team and the lay leaders of the church, who are in close touch with the people, are also a great resource. But in the end, the determination on what to preach cannot be made by a committee, and sooner or later the preacher's decision must be made in the quietness of the preacher's own heart and study.

The key element in my own experience is the question "What is burning in my heart that needs to see the light of day?" This awareness can come from a number of sources. Daily pastoral ministry among the people can give the preacher a clear sense of what they need to hear from the Lord. The preacher's own reading and study can and should lead to subjects burning their way into his heart so thoroughly that the desire to share them with the people becomes extremely powerful. On one occasion I visited Australia for about six weeks. I had, as usual, taken a lot of study materials with me, but I rarely turned to them. My wife and I were entertained in different homes for the duration of the tour, and in each home I picked up books that were lying on the shelves. After about four weeks, I realized that everything I'd been reading dealt with the subject of holiness from a variety of perspectives. I became so intrigued with and concerned about the subject that I knew exactly that my next series had to be about holiness.

Another factor is balance. Every preacher has personal theological preferences. By training or temperament, most preachers will find passages of Scripture that are more appealing to them than others. My own temperamental preferences are the more logically reasoned epistles of Paul. A friend of mine of a somewhat liberal persuasion suggested that I, along with most evangelicals, should really be called a Paulian rather than a Christian, because I seemed to be far more interested in what Paul had to say than what Christ taught. I'm afraid he was right in his observation if not in his conclusion. Like Paul, we need to "proclaim…the whole will of God" (Acts 20:27). We are not free to treat vast areas of Scripture with benign neglect while wearing others thin with our constant attention. The best way to avoid this, I've discovered, is to alternate series of messages from different areas of Scripture. This obviously means maintaining a balance between Old and New Testaments, but it also bears in mind the variety of material found in both Testaments. For example, when I plan a series, I look to see when I last dealt with the Gospels, the Pentateuch, the Pauline epistles, the wisdom literature, the general epistles, the prophets, apocalyptic literature, and the historical books. Then I endeavor, where practical, to alternate between them as well as between the Old and New Testaments. Dividing the Scriptures into their main sections and maintaining a balanced treatment of them helps to keep both preacher and listeners interested.

I also try to change the style of the series. On occasion it is helpful to preach a series of topics that don't necessarily fit into a systematic

---

We are not free to treat vast areas of
Scripture with benign neglect while wearing
others thin with our constant attention.

exposition of a passage of Scripture. This immediately brings up the debate over expository versus topical preaching, so let me address the issue briefly. I firmly believe that preaching should be expository. But by that I do not necessarily mean what some people advocate is the only true exposition of Scripture: a verse-by-verse commentary that works its way through chapter after chapter until the book is finished. Exposition often does take this form; it has great merit, and I have worked my way through many books of Scripture using this method. The problem with this somewhat limited view of exposition is that it tends to downplay the validity of topical preaching.

By *topical preaching* I don't mean the type of preaching that J.I. Packer rightly objects to. He wrote:

> In a topical sermon the text is reduced to a peg on which the speaker hangs his line of thought; the shape and thrust of the message reflect his own best notions of what is good for the people rather than being determined by the text itself. But the only authority that his sermon can then have is the human authority of a knowledgeable person speaking with emphasis and perhaps raising his voice.[4]

If we can define our terms, I think we can come to an understanding that will allow for topical subjects to be dealt with by the exposition of Scripture. By *topical preaching* I do not mean to take a text and use it as a springboard for homiletical gymnastics. I mean to address certain topics that are of interest and concern to the people in such a way that they know exactly what the Word says about them. By *exposition* I mean what I could never express as well as John Stott, so I'll just quote him:

> It is my contention that all true Christian preaching is expository preaching...To expound Scripture is to bring out of the text what is there and expose it to view. The expositor pries open what appears to be closed, makes plain what is obscure, unravels what is knotted and unfolds what is tightly packed. The opposite of exposition is "imposition," which is to impose on the text what is not there.[5]

For example, when I had concluded a twelve-week series of messages based on Deuteronomy called "Enjoying the Good Life," I embarked on a series on holiness called "Life, Liberty, and the Pursuit of Holiness," expounding on the following subjects and passages of Scripture:

1. Holiness and the Character of God (Proverbs 9:10)
2. Holiness and the Condition of Mankind (Isaiah 6:1-13)
3. Holiness and the Contribution of Christ
   (1 Corinthians 1:2, 18-31)
4. Holiness and the Consequences of Redemption
   (1 Peter 1:13-25)
5. Holiness and the Control of the Spirit (Galatians 5:13-26)
6. Holiness and the Consecration of Life (Romans 12:1-2)
7. Holiness and the Challenge of Scripture (John 17:6-19)
8. Holiness and the Commitment to Prayer (1 Timothy 2:1-8)
9. Holiness and the Call of Worship (1 Chronicles 16:23-30)
10. Holiness and the Contemplation of Eternity
    (Revelation 21:1–22:5)

From this outline you will notice a number of things, not least that I suffer periodic attacks of acute alliteration. More importantly, you will note the value of a planned series. We made this outline available to people in advance so they knew what was coming, and contrary to what conventional wisdom might have suggested, the people came with great enthusiasm and brought along other interested people. Second, you will note that while this series was clearly topical, it involved specific exposition. Each message addressed a particular aspect of holiness but always from the perspective of a careful unraveling of a passage of Scripture that deals with the subject. Third, notice that the series ranged over many areas of Scripture, including Old Testament history, wisdom literature, prophets, Pauline epistles, general epistles, and apocalyptic literature. (I'm afraid my liberal friend would have been delighted to pounce on the marked lack of Gospels in the series.)

Varying the length of the series can also add some diversity. This will happen quite naturally when series are built around the traditional

I have become aware of how many biblically illiterate people there are.

Christian events such as Easter and Christmas, which deserve special attention even by those who do not follow the church calendar. In fact, it is usually a good idea to commence sermon planning by blocking off these dates so that series related to the events can be planned first and then other series fitted in. This way the perimeters of each series are spelled out right from the beginning. In some churches there are other events that are especially important. Some preachers will wish to mark Easter, Pentecost, and Christmas but nothing more. Others may want to mark off some vacation time, Mother's Day, the missions festival, Sanctity-of-Life Sunday, Reformation Sunday, Ascension Day, and so on. The fact that some of my readers will not even recognize some of these days indicates how varied are the expectations of different churches and traditions.

The relative merits of inductive versus deductive preaching have been, and continue to be, discussed at great length in some circles. See *Inductive Preaching* by Ralph L. Lewis and Gregg Lewis for a detailed explanation of inductive preaching—as one might have guessed from the title. I personally am much more comfortable with a more deductive approach, but that does not mean I cannot see the merit of using the other approach on occasion to revitalize the preaching.

In the same way, I have more recently rediscovered the value (and the need) for occasional narrative sermons. I see the need because I have become aware of how many biblically illiterate people there are. Preachers used to accurately assume that their congregations knew the basic Bible stories, so they could refer to the stories as illustrations and people would know what they were talking about. Now eyes glaze over, and members of the congregation ask their spouses, "Moses who?" I noticed this particularly in the holiness series when I wanted to talk about "worshipping the Lord in the beauty of holiness." To set the scene for David's exhortation, I felt it was necessary to briefly relate the circumstances that led to David's excitement in finally bringing the ark to Jerusalem. I started out by talking about the lost ark, making reference to Indiana Jones, of course. As a matter of interest, I asked the congregation to indicate if they knew there was a lost ark in the Bible and Noah didn't sail in it. A high proportion of the people indicated they knew far more about Indiana Jones' exploits than the Bible story. But they were intrigued when I adjusted the sermon to tell them the biblical story of the lost ark and used it to lead them to an understanding of its significance for us today. Everybody loves a good story.

Last Easter, instead of preaching a typical sermon on the Resurrection (what greater topic *is* there to preach on?), I decided, as our regular (three times a year) people would be there in force and their knowledge of the story might be sketchy, to tell them the stories of the post-Resurrection appearances to Mary and the disciples. No pulpit, no notes, no outlines…just a half-hour story, taking the roles of the participants, expressing their hidden thoughts, imagining their reactions, portraying their hopelessness, their confusion, their gradual enlightenment, the ecstasy of their discovery, and their infectious delight at the discovery he was alive. There was an air of shared excitement as we left the sanctuary that day.

Everybody loves a good story.

How long should a series last? That's a good question, and I'm afraid I don't think there is a definitive answer. If there is, I have not heard it. I have preached series on Romans, 1 Corinthians, and Genesis that lasted a long time. The Genesis series was made up of fifty messages, one per chapter. The 1 Corinthians series stretched over sixty messages, the last of which was titled "Maranatha," which some of the congregation thought most appropriate. It means "Come, Lord Jesus," and they were unsure which to expect first, the Parousia or the end of the series.

In more recent years, I have tended not to undertake such long series. There can be a tendency for people to become bored, and it is possible that a congregation over that period of time may need another emphasis. This means, of course, that it may not be possible to embark on the task of preaching through a complete book without a break. This is not too important, as most long books of the Bible have natural divisions, and should the preacher break into the flow, he may find that both he and the congregation will return to the rest of the book at a later date with renewed interest. On the other hand, it is always possible to deal with a subject in less detail than most preachers feel necessary. After all, when Paul wrote 1 Corinthians he did not intend that it should be read over a sixty-week period. (With this in mind, when I preached through Romans for the second time I made it in twenty-four sessions, which was considerably quicker than the first time through.) The average length of my series at the present time is nearer eight to twelve weeks, and I have come to the conclusion that, all things considered, this is a good length at which to aim. And if it's a good thing at which to aim, it's a good thing to hit.

If your approach to preaching has been the hand-to-mouth method that may have made preaching more difficult for you, begin to plan ahead and divide your preaching year into bite-sized pieces. The changes and variety will keep you fresh and the congregation alert.

Endnotes

1. James D. Berkley, ed., *Leadership Handbooks of Practical Theology; vol. 1, Word and Worship* (Grand Rapids, Mich.: Baker Books, 1992), 81.

2. J.H. Jowett, *The Preacher, His Life and Work* (Grand Rapids, Mich.: Baker Books, 1977), 114.

3. Arnold Dallimore, *Spurgeon* (Chicago: Moody Press, 1984), 195.

4. Samuel T. Logan, Jr., ed., *The Preacher and Preaching* (Phillipsburg, N.J.: Presbyterian and Reformed Publishing Company, 1986), 4.

5. John R.W. Stott, *Between Two Worlds* (Grand Rapids, Mich.: Wm. B. Eerdmans, 1982), 125-126.

chapter ⓫

....

Preparing a Sermon

Allow me to walk you through the steps I took when preparing a series of eight messages for the period leading up to Easter. The first consideration was to focus on the events in the life of our Lord Jesus leading up to his resurrection. But there was another concern, related to the preaching series I'd just completed. It had been a very challenging series on values, based on the book of Proverbs. I felt that the congregation didn't need another challenging series, but perhaps some words of encouragement and comfort would be appropriate. So I read the fourteenth through the seventeenth chapters of John's Gospel and was immediately impressed with the words "Do not let your hearts be troubled."

The disciples were clearly upset by Jesus' words to them, and they were not coping very well. Jesus, despite his own anguish, was going out of his way to deal with their troubled hearts. My mind went immediately to the people I had ministered to during the last few weeks. In our congregation there is no shortage of troubled hearts stemming from lost jobs, broken marriages, failed romances, business crises, and rebellious children.

Having read and reread the four chapters, I looked for a theme that would do justice to the Scripture under consideration and at the same time ring a bell with the people. I settled on the title "Comfort for Troubled Hearts."

The next thing to do was to divide the four chapters into manageable sections. As I had already worked out that the series needed to last eight weeks, it was clear that each section would be about half a chapter long. I was concerned, however, that to do justice to the text I should avoid unnatural divisions as much as possible. The passages divided quite nicely as follows:

1. John 14:1-14
2. John 14:15-31
3. John 15:1-16
4. John 15:17–16:4
5. John 16:5-15
6. John 16:16-33
7. John 17:1-19
8. John 17:20-26

———— ⟨∘∕∘⟩ ————

There is no shortage of troubled hearts.

———— ⟨∘∕∘⟩ ————

Having established the divisions of the passage under consideration, the next thing to do was to identify the theme of each one, linking it, if possible, to the overarching theme of the series. This required looking for key words and concepts in each passage. For instance, an obvious emphasis in the first passage is "Trust in God; trust also in me." In fact the "Do not let your hearts be troubled" injunction is clearly related to "Trust in God; trust also in me." The title, therefore, that came to mind was "Comfort Through Trust." This identified the passage with the overall theme of comfort but also clearly underlined the emphasis of the verses under consideration, showing that comfort and trust are inextricably bound up in each other. After establishing this subtitle, I read through the following passages looking for a similar title for each one. There is an advantage to developing some kind of symmetry in the titles without forcing your ideas onto the text. So the outline of the series developed as follows:

1. Comfort Through Trust (John 14:1-14)
2. Comfort Through Love (John 14:15-31)
3. Comfort Through Relationship (John 15:1-16)

4. Comfort Through Trials (John 15:17–16:4)

5. Comfort Through the Spirit (John 16:5-15)

6. Comfort Through Grief (John 16:16-33)

7. Comfort Through Prayer (John 17:1-19)

8. Comfort Through Unity (John 17:20-26)

In principle, the advantage of having an eight-week ministry outline is that the preacher knows the general direction to be taken for the next period of time, and the staff involved in worship preparation can set to work knowing where they are heading.

In addition, having established the outline early, we can publicize the series. So in this case, as soon as the titles for the series were established, I met with one of our graphic artists, explained what I intended to do, and asked her to design a poster that we would display in strategic parts of the church. I checked back with her a few days later, and she said, "I like the idea of comfort in trouble and I imagined something like this." She handed me a rough sketch of a large gnarled hand holding a tiny infant's hand. "I think we should use a warm, gentle color for the poster," she added, "maybe rose or pink. This should convey comfort for troubled hearts." This may seem like unnecessary attention to detail, and I agree that the church will probably survive very well without pink or rose posters as, no doubt, did the churches Paul founded. Moreover, not every pastor is as blessed as I am with a large group of talented and gifted people, but note two important things. First, we should use all manner of legitimate means of conveying a message and creating interest. And second, we should be giving all the talented people in the congregation the opportunity to bring their uniqueness to bear on the communication of the truth. I assure you that our graphic artist feels herself part of the ministry, and many people in the congregation have been alerted to the good news of comfort for troubled hearts by her work, even before I have uttered a word from the Word.

Once the structure of the series has been determined, I have found a certain relaxation of spirit. As it is no longer necessary to spend a lot of time wondering what to preach about, the time can be more profitably spent concentrating on the development of the series as outlined. The

Once the structure of the series has been determined, I have found a certain relaxation of spirit.

———— ⬥⬥⬥ ————

worship team sets to work thinking about the various elements of the service related to the subject, which adds to an air of expectancy in the pews. The laypeople who volunteer to help research some of the topics busy themselves in libraries or search through clippings, and the musicians start to practice the music that will open hearts and minds to the Word. It's as if a great engine is started up and begins to hum industriously as all the interlocking parts do their job.

Bearing in mind that "cases are made in chambers," the work of crafting the sermon from the appointed passage must begin in earnest. For me this means reading and rereading the text until it is thoroughly ingrained in my mind. I could not say it is memorized, but it is close. The theme of the passage has already been identified, and so the next thing is to collate all the material in the passage that relates to the theme.

In the case of the first message, the theme was comfort through trust. I used all the sources available to help me understand as much as possible what was in the mind of the writer as, under the guidance of the Holy Spirit, he wrote his Gospel. I perused Bible dictionaries, commentaries, and the like. Kittel's massive *Theological Dictionary of the New Testament* has been a great help, as have the four volumes of the revised *International Standard Bible Encyclopedia.* For the series under consideration, I read and digested various commentaries on John's Gospel such as Leon Morris', George Beasley-Murray's, and Merrill Tenney's.

As I read, I jotted down notes in a notebook especially reserved for preserving the results of this kind of study. For years I used to scribble my notes on odd pieces of paper which, of course, have long ago disappeared. That was, no doubt, an appropriate end for most of them, but I have to think that some of the work could have been preserved for future reference.

I was interested to notice that the word for "troubled" is *tarasso*, which is used in the disputed verse, John 5:4, to describe the water at the pool of Bethesda as being "stirred up." But what interested me more was the discovery that Jesus is described by John as being "troubled" on three occasions: in 11:33; 12:27; and 13:21. This, of course, required some thought as to how he who was himself troubled could require his disciples not to be troubled. *Tarasso*, I also discovered, means "to be disturbed, agitated, and confused." So I had done what was necessary as far as *troubled* was concerned, and that was to define it and illustrate it from the text.

It was then necessary to identify why the disciples were troubled. This was not hard to discover. I jotted the following in my notebook:

> **1.** All troubled by being "shamed" through the foot washing.
>
> **2.** Peter troubled because of predicted denial.
>
> **3.** Thomas troubled because he was confused.
>
> **4.** Philip troubled because he wanted more than he was getting.
>
> **5.** Jesus troubled because he knew what was coming.

Not much time was necessary to see the very real similarity between the troubling circumstances of the Lord and his disciples and those of many of the people I would address. When I felt I had enough raw material to establish the trouble the people in the text were going through and the means to apply it to the contemporary congregation, I turned my attention to the next part of the text: "Trust in God; trust also in me."

A few days before I started studying this passage, I had read John Claypool's book *The Preaching Event* and had been particularly intrigued by his treatment of the Eden event in which our forefather and foremother showed a marked preference for distrusting God rather than trusting him. He told a brilliant story about identical twin brothers who, through totally unwarranted distrust, had ruined their lives and divided a community, only to discover after twenty years the magnitude of their mistake and the awful consequences to which many people had been subjected. Fortunately I had made a note of this insight and illustration, so I knew where to find it to refresh my memory. This enabled me to develop further insights into people's innate tendency to distrust God, the awesome consequences of their distrust, and their need to learn to trust and find the comfort they so earnestly desire. I mention this to show how important it is to preserve the insights gained from reading so they can be readily utilized when most needed, and also to demonstrate that it is perfectly appropriate to benefit from the work of others, particularly if we are courteous enough to identify our sources and express our appreciation.

I then turned my attention to what it means to "trust in God." Given that we all have a tendency to distrust, I wondered what is in the passage to encourage trust. I didn't have to look very long for answers. The passage yielded the following information, which I duly noted in my notebook:

Jesus expected his disciples to trust God and him for these reasons:

1. His words had been shown to be true.

2. Even if that was not conceded, his works were irrefutable.

3. His integrity, therefore, was not in question.

4. Therefore, his statements about heaven were encouraging.

5. His promise to return was categorical.

6. The prospect of being with him would be worth trusting in.

7. In any case, what better options were available to them?

Once again, I felt there was more raw material available than I would have time to use, so I turned my attention to the last part of the passage.

Jesus' statement about "greater things" has always intrigued me, and I noted that the reason his disciples would function at this level was because he was going to the Father. I assumed this was "shorthand" for the "gift of the Spirit" and reasoned that Jesus was promising the remarkable equipping of the church that would lead not to greater things than raising the dead (that would be a tall order) but greater things in terms of millions of believers over the millennia stretching to the outermost parts of the earth. This work, accomplished through the Holy Spirit, continues the work that Christ began and far exceeds the limitations of his self-imposed incarnation. Thus his disciples would be greatly comforted by their sense of noble calling and adequate resources.

Preserve the insights gained from
reading so they can be readily
utilized when most needed.

———————— ◦/◦/◦ ————————

Then there was the wonderful statement about effective prayer—not, I noted, carte blanche to ask for any old thing and persuade oneself to believe it's guaranteed, but rather that prayer in God's name and for God's glory would lead to definite answers. What comfort!

By this time I had no shortage of material or notes, and it was time to bring a little order into relative chaos, so outline time had arrived.

Some preachers have found it helpful to write their sermons, and there are obvious advantages to this approach. Thoughts that have been written down can be polished and made more precise. A clear sense of progression of thought can be identified, and no doubt the very act of writing helps to instill the thoughts into the preacher's mind. Some preachers write their sermons then memorize the manuscript. Others feel confident that they know it thoroughly enough to leave the manuscript at home; while still others take it with them and read it verbatim.

To each his own. I do none of these. I prefer to outline my sermon clearly and in some detail, to have it firmly in my mind, and always to have it in front of me when I preach. The main reason for this is that I preach the message four times, and sometimes during the third or fourth service, I have the most horrible feeling that I've already said what I'm about to say. I *have* just said it, of course, but it was in the previous service. Having an outline keeps me on the straight and narrow, but it does not tie me to the lectern to the extent that I lose sight of the people before me. In addition, giving a copy of the outline to members of the congregation assists them in following the train of thought, gives them something to take home for further study either on their own or in their small groups, and gives them a feeling that they are expected to concentrate on what is being said and even to take further notes.

Having an outline keeps me on the straight and narrow, but it does not tie me to the lectern to the extent that I lose sight of the people before me.

———— ✦ ————

An outline is to notes what menus are to food being prepared for a banquet. Scattered as they are around the kitchen or the study, both need to be brought together in some coherent fashion. Looking over my notes, which were scattered and unrelated, I needed a structure for the sermon similar to the structure I had for the series. I decided that the three main points would be as follows:

I. Troubled hearts

II. Trusting hearts

III. Triumphant hearts

Having settled on this structure, I then began to sort out the raw material under these three main headings. This was the result:

I. Troubled hearts

A. *The Savior's troubled heart*

1. Confronting the pain of despair (John 11:33)

2. Facing the horror of crucifixion (John 12:27)

3. Recognizing the brutality of betrayal (John 13:21)

B. *The disciples' troubled hearts*

1. Because of disgrace (John 13:17)

2. Because of desertion (John 13:30)

3. Because of denial (John 13:38)

4. Because of disillusionment (John 14:5, 8)

II. Trusting hearts

A. *The disaster of distrust*

1. Humans were made to trust God.

2. God's trustworthiness called into question (Genesis 3:1)

3. Disintegration and disillusionment result.

4. God's commitment to restoring the relationship (John 14:1)

B. *The basis of belief*

1. Jesus made his point.

   a) *By his words: "I tell you the truth" (John 14:12)*

   b) *By his works: "What I have been doing" (John 14:12)*

2. Jesus stated his position (John 14:6).

   a) *I am the way.*

   b) *I am the truth.*

   c) *I am the life.*

3. Jesus outlined his promise (John 14:2-4).

   a) *The Father's house has many rooms.*

   b) *I'm going to prepare one for you.*

   c) *I will come back for you.*

   d) *You will be with me.*

III. Triumphant hearts

A. *The comfort of knowing God in Christ (John 14:7)*

B. *The comfort of knowing adequate resources (John 14:12)*

1. The principle of faith

2. The power of the Spirit: "Because I am going…"

C. *The comfort of knowing answered prayer (John 14:13-14)*

1. Prayer that seeks God's glory

2. Prayer offered in Christ's name

Only the introduction and conclusion needed to be added to the outline. In this instance, because the message was the first in a new series, I needed an introduction not only for the message but also for the series.

Right before I got up to preach, the congregation had witnessed a dramatized reading of parts of John 13 that graphically set the scene of the upper room, so people had a point of connection. All that was needed by way of introduction was for me to say, "Jesus, knowing what lay ahead of him, spent the waning hours of his life with his disciples. It was a difficult time for them, and they became deeply troubled. Jesus' response was to tell them, 'Trust in God; trust also in me; do not let your hearts be troubled.' Easier said than done, but still the way for troubled hearts to find comfort."

So much for a brief outline and introduction, but what about a conclusion? I have found it helpful by way of application, and if you like, as a "parting shot," to give people "points to ponder." These are included in the outline and are usually identified and repeated as the final words of the sermon. This way the application is reinforced, and provocative ideas profitable for further thought are provided. So the outline concluded with the usual points to ponder and advance warning of what to expect next week, as follows:

Points to ponder:

Do I have a troubled heart? What do I need to make it a trusting heart?

Next week:

"Comfort Through Love" (John 14:15-31)

Because I spend time studying the passage in some detail, most of the material is fixed in my mind, so I find I can remember the thrust of the message without more detailed notes than the outline. The only difference between my outline and that in the hands of the congregation is that I make careful notes of any quotations and illustrations I plan to use. This brings me to the final aspect of the hard work of preparing the outlined sermon: finding and fitting in the necessary "color" to bring the sermon alive and make it memorable. Let's face it, preachers: It's the illustrations and the stories the hearers remember, even if they don't always remember the point. But more of this later.

I have made no specific reference to the place of prayer in sermon preparation, not because I don't believe in it or because it is unnecessary, but rather because I find that as I immerse myself in the Word, wrestle with its concepts, and apply it to myself, I am borne along in a spirit of prayer and worship that is almost automatic. Moreover, as I come across concepts that are hard to understand or hard to explain, the natural recourse is to pray for insight and to request from God the strength and ability to complete the task. Should you not find this to be your experience, I encourage you to stop periodically in your preparations to talk to the Lord about what he has been saying to you.

Remember, if cases are made in chambers, it is equally true that sermons are crafted in studies.

As I immerse myself in the Word, wrestle with its concepts, and apply it to myself, I am borne along in a spirit of prayer and worship that is almost automatic.

chapter 12

....

Pointers on Proclamation

My philosophy of preaching, if I may grace my attempts with such a grandiose term, is based on a delightful passage of Scripture recorded in Nehemiah 8. It tells the story of Ezra, the scribe who was encouraged by the people to bring out and read from the Book of the Law as part of the Feast of Tabernacles celebration. He stood on a pulpit of wood, specially erected for the purpose, so everybody could see him, and "he read aloud from daybreak till noon" (Nehemiah 8:3). This is a verse which all preachers should memorize as a response to people who grumble about the length of their sermons. But while the length of the reading was impressive, it was what the people did about the reading that's of great importance to preachers in all ages. Ezra enrolled the help of a number of people (Levites) whose unpronounceable names are listed for our edification. They "read from the Book of the Law of God, making it clear and giving the meaning so that the people could understand what was being read" (Nehemiah 8:8).

Presumably they took turns in this "preach-a-thon." But even then they had not completed their work, for we read the following: "Then Nehemiah the governor, Ezra the priest and scribe, and the Levites who were instructing the people said to them all, 'This day is sacred to the Lord your God. Do not mourn or weep.' For all the people had been weeping as they listened to the words of the Law. Nehemiah said, 'Go and enjoy choice food and sweet drinks, and send some to those who have nothing prepared. This day is sacred to our Lord. Do not grieve, for the joy of the Lord is your strength' " (Nehemiah 8:9-10).

Making the Word clear is the

essence of proclamation.

—⟨∘⟩∘⟨∘⟩—

For many years these verses have served as the basis for my attempts at preaching. Let us take a closer look at the approach these preachers took.

four Basic Ingredients

First they read from the Word, "making it clear." Making the Word clear is the essence of proclamation. Then they worked hard at "giving the meaning," which is another way of saying they got into explanation. Their explanation was not purely academic but essentially practical, directed as it was "so that the people could understand." In other words, this was application. The people, however, still needed to be told exactly how to go about the implementation of the Word in their unique circumstances, so they were told, "Go and enjoy choice food and sweet drinks, and send something to those who have nothing prepared" (verse 10). That's implementation.

We would do well in all our preaching to keep these four things in mind:

1. Proclamation
2. Explanation
3. Application
4. Implementation

Getting Listeners' Attention

Let me suggest some practical pointers on the subject of proclamation. What exactly are we trying to do? The answer to that all-important question is that we are concerned with handling the Word of God in such a way that people who hear it will know what to do about it. But first we have to get people in the kind of situation where they are likely to hear the Word. In many parts of the world the days are gone when people surrendered themselves without a murmur of protest to being preached to, or at, depending on their frame of mind.

Even so, there is still a sizable number of people in the American church. Many of them are committed Christians who need to be nourished by the Word, and quite a few of them are non-Christians who need to be born again. Healthy churches always keep both kinds of people in mind, and alert preachers keep both groups of people in their sights. In addition, the modern preacher must not just think of preaching to church attenders. Today's preacher needs to look for, and if necessary create, opportunities for preaching the Word outside the four walls of the sanctuary to those whose presence may never grace a pew. In my early days of preaching, I probably preached more often outside churches than inside. (This probably is a fair commentary on what the church, as a whole, thought of my preaching!)

We are concerned with handling the Word of God in such a way that people who hear it will know what to do about it.

So I learned to preach in the pubs and clubs and coffee bars of England and on street corners that had been bombed during World War II. Most of my preaching nowadays takes place inside a church, but I still rejoice in opportunities to address businessmen's clubs, to speak on university campuses, to give "inspirational" after-dinner speeches, and to take advantage of whatever other opportunities present themselves. When I preach, wherever I preach, whatever I preach, I always keep in mind the people who are not familiar either with the church or the gospel. Those who have been brought by their friends, who have come because of our television outreach, or who have wandered in out of curiosity are not about to sit and listen if they aren't interested in what I have to say.

Modern ears have been trained to

listen to sound bites, not sermons.

———— ⟞⟪⟫⟞ ————

Modern cultures provide a bewildering variety of options for people. There is no shortage of voices claiming their attention. The demands of work and the opportunities for play are so great that the main problem for a lot of people is trying to fit everything into their busy schedules. This being the case, preachers need to face up to the unpleasant fact that they must compete for the attention of those they endeavor to reach. To make matters worse, modern preachers not only cannot assume that people will gladly lend them their ears, they must also reckon with the fact that modern ears have been trained to listen to sound bites, not sermons. Twenty-first-century preachers need to know how to get people's attention and then what to do with it and how to keep it. But concentrating on getting people's attention produces its own problems for the preacher.

god-centered and people-related

Spurgeon said in his *Lectures to My Students*, "In order to get attention the first golden rule is, always say something worth hearing." Then he added, "Nobody sleeps when he expects to hear something to his advantage. I have heard of some very strange things, but I never did hear of a person going to sleep while a will was being read in which he expected a legacy, neither have I heard of a prisoner going to sleep while the judge was summing up, and his life was hanging in jeopardy."[1] In other words, people in those situations know they are going to hear something significant to them, and they are all ears. So if we want to get people's attention, we must talk about what they are interested in.

Two things must be kept in balance. While preaching must always be people-related, it cannot qualify as preaching unless it is God-centered. Now that's a rather obvious statement, but like a lot of obvious statements it bears repeating. I see a current preaching trend that concerns me. It has to do with what may become a lack of proper balance between these two elements.

As I have already indicated, I recognize there are many different ways of preaching. There are all kinds of starting points, and there are many valid ways of communicating the truth. But for there to be a proper balance, we must insist on the centrality of God in all our preaching. John Piper made this point powerfully in his book *The Supremacy of God in Preaching*. On the other hand, if our preaching is not people-related, it will fail to measure up to the standard set by Ezra and his colleagues, but more important, it will fail abysmally to accomplish what preaching is intended to accomplish. If preaching does not deal with life situations by presenting the Lord of life as the key to life, it is inadequate.

My concern about some of the modern trends is that the approach appears to be dangerously close to being people-centered and God-related. While modern preaching demonstrates a most commendable and appropriate insight into people's hurts and needs and attempts to address them by showing that God is concerned with meeting their needs, I fear that sometimes people get the impression that God exists to meet their needs. If God exists primarily to meet people's needs, he is in danger of becoming in many people's minds nothing more than the "needs meeter in the sky." People who are attracted to God on this basis are notoriously reluctant to progress further into a relationship with him that realistically could be called discipleship. Moreover, while they relate very well to God as long as he meets their needs (which may or may not be needs and can very easily be whims and caprices), they quickly become disillusioned with him and turn to other gurus when he fails to come up with the answers they expect.

While preaching must always be people-related, it cannot qualify as preaching unless it is God-centered.

Each God-centered, people-related sermon should accomplish three things:

1. It must *instruct* people about who God is and what he has said.
2. It must *identify* with the human condition.
3. It must *indicate* an appropriate behavioral response.

I am intrigued by Paul's ministry in Thessalonica. We are not told the particular needs Paul encountered and addressed when he arrived there, but we do know that his ministry was singularly effective. After his very short visit, a church was born that Paul characterized as a model for churches in the surrounding area. The reason for this, he stated, was that the people had "turned to God from idols to serve the living and true God, and to wait for his Son from heaven" (1 Thessalonians 1:9-10). Whatever the starting point of Paul's preaching, there can be no doubt it was God-centered because it produced God-centered believers. God was the focus of their attention. They had turned to God and were eager to serve him as they waited for his Son. In light of the fact that their lives and testimonies were so exemplary, it is reasonable to assume that their needs had also been met. All preachers wish to see the fruit of their labor in people who once were self-absorbed but now have become devoted believers and willing servants of the living God. For this to happen, the focus of preaching must be carefully maintained: God-centered and people-related.

All preachers wish to see the fruit of their labor in people who once were self-absorbed but now have become devoted believers and willing servants of the living God.

Attention-grabbing subjects

Over the thirty-two years of my pastorate, times have changed. For example, if I had announced in the early days that I would be teaching Paul's Epistle to the Romans, all kinds of people would have shown up. Now the people on the periphery (and preachers should always have these people in mind unless they're content to preach to the converted in order to convince the convinced) are much less likely to show interest in either Paul or the Romans. But they are interested in "felt needs." This does not mean they're necessarily unconcerned about "real needs," but the preacher's job is to get them from their interest in the former to an identification of the latter—to move them from what is itching to what is causing the itch and to scratch it at the same time.

For example, recently I was concerned to show from Jesus' teaching that there are some actions we should take even though things are happening in our lives that we cannot control. I was meeting more and more people who were experiencing difficulties in their lives because they had been (or believed they had been) abused and victimized. They believed that life had been unfair, that circumstances or fate or God or all of the above had dealt unkindly with them, and that there was nothing for them to do but feel resentful and hurt about it. I had decided to preach a series on the parables recorded in Luke, but I knew the messages must relate to the major "need button" that so many were wearing. So the series was titled "What to Do While Your Life Is Happening." This stimulated a lot of interest that I'm afraid "A Series of Talks on the Parables" would have failed to do.

If preaching does not deal with life situations by presenting the Lord of life as the key to life, it is inadequate.

In the example of the previous chapter, the messages were born out of a concern to address certain "felt needs." But in a later series of messages, I was compelled from my own reading in Hebrews to teach some of the major lessons that had caught my interest. I was gripped by this verse: "Let us then approach the throne of grace with confidence, so that we may receive mercy and find grace to help us in our time of need" (Hebrews 4:16).

Bearing in mind the necessity to grip people's attention, I developed the series as follows:

where to find help

1. Where to Find Help Cleaning Up Your Life (Hebrews 1:1-4)
2. Where to Find Help Coping With Your Fears (Hebrews 2:14-18)
3. Where to Find Help Facing Up to Your Frustrations (Hebrews 4:1-13)
4. Where to Find Help Dealing With Your Temptations (Hebrews 4:14-16)
5. Where to Find Help Seeing Beyond Your Problems (Hebrews 5:7–6:12)
6. Where to Find Help Handling Your Insecurities (Hebrews 6:13-20)
7. Where to Find Help Clearing Your Conscience (Hebrews 9:1-14)
8. Where to Find Help Strengthening Your Faith (Hebrews 10:19-39)
9. Where to Find Help Running Your Race (Hebrews 12:1-13)
10. Where to Find Help Developing Your Worship (Hebrews 12:14-29)
11. Where to Find Help Improving Your Attitudes (Hebrews 13:1-6)
12. Where to Find Help Following Your Leaders (Hebrews 13:7-25)

Holding people's Attention

It is one thing to grab attention. It is another to hold it, particularly in a culture in which many people are more accustomed to sound bites than to getting their teeth into something. This means that the preacher must not only use interesting material, he must also communicate it in an interesting way. The demeanor of the communicator is a big factor. If the preacher gives the impression of being less than gripped by the subject, it will hardly be surprising if the congregation finds it less than arresting. Dr. D. Martyn Lloyd-Jones, the late Welsh preacher, wrote in *Preaching and Preachers:*

> The preacher must never be dull, he must never be boring; he should never be what is called "heavy"…I would say that a dull preacher is a contradiction in terms; if he is dull he is not a preacher.[2]

This we will look into in the next chapter.

Endnotes

1. Charles H. Spurgeon, *Lectures to My Students* (London: Marshall Pickering, first published 1954, reissued 1989), 130, 138.

2. D. Martyn Lloyd-Jones, *Preaching and Preachers* (London: Hodder and Stoughton, 1971), 87.

———————— ⎯⎯ ————————

The preacher must not only use interesting

material, he must also communicate

it in an interesting way.

———————— ⎯⎯ ————————

chapter ⑬

Developing Introductions

At the risk of getting things back-to-front, I usually develop my introduction to the sermon after the rest is complete. I admit there was a time I would simply stand up and say, "Would you open your Bibles, please?" While that is perfectly valid, it is not exactly attention-grabbing for a lot of people, particularly if they haven't brought a Bible—or if they can see one in the pew in front of them but are afraid to pick it up because they have no idea where to find the first Epistle of Peter and are not about to demonstrate the fact by fumbling. So putting a little thought into introductions can go a long way. The opening paragraph of my outline would not always be the introduction to the sermon, because introductions are often most effective if they contain an element of surprise.

W.E. Sangster wrote:

> [The preacher] has the awful task of making the word of God live to men and women who have been busy all the week seeking the bread of this life and who, even in the sanctuary, find it hard to keep their minds on God and holy things. He must help them in every wholesome way he can. If he can get an arresting beginning, he may have their awed attention the whole time and be able to hide the truth of God deep in their hearts.[1]

Introductions are often most effective
if they contain an element of surprise.

―――――――――――――― ⚬⚬⚬ ――――――――――――――

The way to up

The Keswick Convention in the north of England is an annual event. When I was young, it was the British Super Bowl of evangelicalism. My family attended every year just on Wednesday, because my dad had a store and that was half-day closing day. It was a bore. I used to sit there on a hard bench in the big tent on a warm summer afternoon, thinking of lots of places I'd rather be. On Wednesdays the subject was always the lordship of Christ. In those days I approached that subject with a considerable degree of trepidation, so you can imagine my annual frame of mind as convention time rolled around and once more I deposited my unwilling youthfulness on an unyielding bench, knowing full well I would be exposed to unpalatable truth.

On one occasion I was sitting there wondering how long an hour was going to last and paying such scant attention to the proceedings that I was unaware the meeting had begun. Suddenly a voice bellowed, "The way to up is down!" There was a sort of fluttering among the people as when doves in a cote suspect a cat might be in the vicinity. I looked up, and there was a tall man with wavy gray hair—at least that's how he looked to me as a kid all those years ago. He just stood there looking sternly at the people. There was a very long, dramatic pause. I became quite nervous. Then he bellowed, "The way to down is up!"

That introduction was unforgettable, as is evidenced by the fact that I still remember it. Here I sit in my seventies, more than fifty-five years later, remembering as if it were yesterday the opening lines of a sermon I did not want to hear. I found out subsequently that the preacher's name was Donald Grey Barnhouse. But more important, I discovered the principle he taught that day. He gave an exposition of what had been stated more prosaically by Peter: " 'God opposes the proud but gives grace to the humble.' Humble yourselves, therefore, under God's mighty hand, that he may lift you up in due time" (1 Peter 5:5b-6).

To my mind this was a classic introduction, because it not only grabbed my attention but was succinct and sharply focused as it encapsulated an entire message in memorable form and worded a rather abstract, anachronistic expression in arresting modern terms. No, we are not all called Barnhouse, but we can all work on our introductions.

I deposited my unwilling youthfulness on an unyielding bench, knowing full well I would be exposed to unpalatable truth.

Tell us a story

It's humbling for preachers to bear in mind how little people remember of what they say, and even more disconcerting when they realize the things people find memorable. They remember your mistakes, and if your teeth fly out, they will never forget that. But the good news is they like and tend to remember good stories. So preachers should think of stories that will not only aid memory but will also serve as attention-grabbing introductions, entrances to the structure of their sermons.

One day I started a series of talks on motivation with this story. Jill and I arrived in Kimberley, South Africa, and were met at the airport by a little lady whom we had not previously met. Fortunately, she recognized us, and as we were getting our bags, she surprised me by saying, "Would you like to see the hole?"

And so, being British, I said, "I beg your pardon?" If I'd been American I would have said, "Huh?" I had no idea what she was talking about, but being terribly British and excruciatingly polite, I

It's humbling for preachers to bear in mind how little people remember of what they say, and even more disconcerting when they realize the things people find memorable.

───── ⌘ ─────

said, "We would love to see the hole. Thank you very much indeed."

She said, "Would you like to see where you're staying first, or would you like to go to the hole immediately?"

Recognizing that her enthusiasm knew no bounds, I said, "Immediately. Let's go right away!"

As we were driving along, she said, "It's the biggest man-made hole in the world, you know."

I replied quite truthfully, "No. I didn't know that."

"Oh, yes," she replied with great enthusiasm, "and it was dug with very primitive implements."

"Like what?" I inquired.

"Oh," she said, "little hand shovels and leather buckets and a system of pulleys. And it's a mile in circumference, and hundreds of feet deep."

She went on, hardly stopping to take a breath. "It was awful. There was rioting and famine and there was plague and there was murder. It was awful. But people traveled from all over the world to participate in digging this hole!"

It was obvious to me by this time that the little lady assumed I knew all about this phenomenon, and I was intent on hiding my ignorance as long as possible. But by this time I was getting really interested.

She said, "It used to be a hill, you know."

Now that really got me. "Used to be a hill?"

She said, "Yes. Indeed. It used to be a hill."

By this time we'd arrived, and sure enough, there was no hill, just a hole. One mile in circumference. Hundreds of feet deep. My curiosity was totally stimulated by this time, so I asked, "Why would people come from all over the world to start digging on top of a hill to make the biggest hole in the world in the middle of nowhere?"

She was eager to explain. "Well, it is very simple, really. Some little boys were playing on the hill one day, throwing pebbles to one another. An old gentleman walking past saw the sun glint on one of the pebbles and he caught it, examined it, and immediately recognized it. A diamond. The Kimberley Diamond Mine was born!"

And that's how you turn a hill into the biggest hole in the world. Diamonds lying around do tend to motivate.

I've told the story many times, and people are usually intrigued by it. Of course, we're not called to be intriguing raconteurs, so we have to make a point from the story. In this case I wanted to point out that when adequately motivated, for good or evil, human beings are capable of remarkable feats, but when insufficiently motivated they will almost always live far below their potential. It's hard to imagine circumstances under which people could have been persuaded to leave home and kindred, travel to the African veldt, and endure amazing hardship and danger simply to dig a hole. But greed being what it is, and the desire to get rich quick being a powerful motivator, they went, proving to me without doubt that one of the most important factors in life is motivation. The series then developed the theme of motivation from a study of Paul's autobiographical passages, which allow a look into the head of the great apostle to see what motivated him, what made him tick.

We're not called to be intriguing raconteurs,

so we have to make a point from the story.

wavelengths

John Stott quips that many people regard preachers as "six days invisible and one day incomprehensible." My guess is that the two are linked. Some preachers literally stay sequestered in their studies so that they have little contact with people where they live. Others do it metaphorically in that they spend all their time wading through the murky depths of theology and philosophy without ever setting foot in the mundane shallows where most people live their lives. Both sets of preachers will have difficulty understanding how people think, which means their listeners will have difficulty understanding what preachers say. Invisible can mean incomprehensible. Craig Skinner stated bluntly, "Any speaker who assumes that his audience thinks and feels exactly as he does will always be wrong."[2] Preachers must keep in touch with the world of their people, not at the expense of study but always with relevance in mind.

This is particularly important when introductions are being crafted. The introduction not only serves to introduce a topic of interest to the people, thereby getting their attention, but it also serves to introduce the preacher in a way that will intrigue the listener. "This guy understands where I'm living." "I'm glad to know this preacher isn't living on cloud nine while I'm struggling in pit twelve." "Oh, he knows about that movie I saw and didn't understand." "Ah, he has an opinion on what the president said this week." "I wonder what he thinks." All these reactions and many more can and should be buzzing in the congregation's minds after an appropriate beginning.

For example, during the 1992 presidential election, Dan Quayle, the vice president, made a critical comment about Murphy Brown having a baby out of wedlock. The fact that Murphy Brown, a TV character, did not exist in no way inhibited the eruption of a furious debate on the subject of family values. All that was necessary to get people's attention the next week, and in fact to embark on an eight-week series on values, was my opening comment, "Murphy and Dan have been having problems this week." The congregation laughed, some a little nervously, and we were on our way to a statement about the necessity of values, an explanation of what we mean by values, an exploration of

People are always interested in relationships.

the way we arrive at values, and an evaluation of the values that significantly determine our lifestyles.

I am particularly concerned about the fact that in the church whenever we talk about relationships, we almost always deal with marital situations, despite the fact that up to a third of the adult population, and therefore a third of many congregations, is single. So on one occasion I read from a questionnaire sent out by a personal introduction service. This certainly grabbed the attention of the singles, but it was also interesting to married folks who had little idea of the particular stresses and strains of single life in the modern world. For example, here are some of the questions raised in the questionnaire:

1. Are you in a dead-end relationship or in a relationship of convenience?
2. Are you tired of meeting people who in the beginning say they are everything that you want, then you find out within six months that they are totally different?
3. Are you tired of having your intelligence insulted by the games you have to play to meet someone special?
4. Are you tired of meeting men/women with whom you fall in love and then discover that you are not the only one in their life?
5. Do you feel unsafe with the conventional methods of meeting people?

It will not be difficult to move from this sampling of the issues confronting people in their search for authentic relationships to a discussion of the factors that make for the deep relationships for which the human heart craves. People are always interested in relationships.

It's time I came to a conclusion on the subject of introductions. My son Pete was invited to preach in his seminary chapel shortly before graduation, an honor afforded to only two students each year. So his proud parents went to listen while looking appropriately humble. After a rather tepid introduction from one of the professors, Pete strode to the microphone, all 6 feet 5 inches of him, and without hesitation said, "You never get a second chance to make a first impression." It wasn't original, but it was powerful, and it is true of introductions. You don't get a second chance to make a first impression, so take the one chance you get, and make it work.

Endnotes

1. W.E. Sangster, *The Craft of the Sermon* (London: Epworth Press, 1954), 126.

2. Craig Skinner, *The Teaching Ministry of the Pulpit* (Grand Rapids, Mich.: Baker Books, 1973), 75.

chapter ⑭

Including Explanations and Applications

We noted earlier that Ezra and his friends "read from the Book of the Law…making it clear and giving the meaning." Some scholars suggest that this means they read a paragraph at a time and then the Levites circulated among the crowd and carefully got into what we have called explanation and application. To adopt this approach some Sunday morning would certainly add freshness to the preaching, although the congregation might be alarmed if the preacher stopped after a few minutes and sat down, and then deacons descended on them from all corners of the sanctuary. Better, perhaps, to content ourselves with applying the principles to our modern scene and concentrating on what it takes to explain and apply the Word, although there is no substitute for personal application. I think it was Spurgeon who said, "Preaching is like throwing a bucket of water at a row of bottles. Some of the water goes in some of the bottles. But personal application ensures that all the bottles are filled up." (If Spurgeon didn't say it, I'm sure he would have if he'd thought of it.) What can be done from the pulpit to ensure that as many people as possible understand as much as can be expected?

The perils of communication

As Dr. Deborah Tannen has pointed out in her best-selling books *That's Not What I Meant* and *You Just Don't Understand,* communication is a perilous business. In the latter book, she concentrated on the different ways that males and females communicate. Her objective was to "make sense of the seemingly senseless misunderstandings that

Preachers should think about what they say, what people think about what they say, and how to answer them.

———— ⌘ ————

haunt our relationships, and show that a man and a woman can interpret the same conversation differently, even when there is no apparent misunderstanding."[1] I came to the conclusion after reading her book that all male preachers who speak to large numbers of women would do well to delve into its pages and gain from her insights.

Misunderstandings happen. One day a golfer said to his partner, "I got a new set of golf clubs for my wife."

His partner looked up and said, "Boy, I wish I could make a trade like that."

At the risk of spoiling a little joke by taking it too seriously (a joke, incidentally, more likely to elicit laughs from men than women), let me suggest why that "misunderstanding" occurred. The first man was probably happily married. He was excited his wife was taking up golf and was pleased to give her a present to show his love and to encourage her in her new hobby. The other man was probably unhappily married, was more interested in golf than his wife, and was primarily thinking about ways to make his own lot in life more pleasant. The point is that what we hear is not necessarily what was intended by the speaker. What is "heard" may have more to do with the hearer's preoccupations and presuppositions than with the speaker's intentions.

On one memorable occasion, a man came to me and said, "OK, what are you pro-life people going to do about it?" I had no idea what he was talking about, so I asked him to clarify whatever was concerning him. He then referred to a statement I had made in an effort to bring home the force of Jesus' statement that he would not abandon us as orphans. I had said, "We are all familiar with the images of starving, abandoned children in Somalia, with the faces of HIV-infected orphans in

Romania, and with the desperate situation of unwanted babies born as a result of organized rape in Bosnia and Herzegovina." Unfortunately, his militant pro-choice position had been so dominant in his thinking that he had sat through the sermon fuming over what he perceived to be a connection between pro-life groups in America and the activities of Serbian, Croatian, and Muslim soldiers in what is left of Yugoslavia. He spent so much time fuming that he missed the whole point of what I was trying to say. But that's all part of the perils of communication. This does not mean we should throw up our hands in despair. It points out that we must stay sensitive to the problem and committed to making it as hard as possible for people to find ways to misunderstand us.

———————— ⟨⟨⟨⟩⟩⟩ ————————

What we hear is not necessarily what was intended by the speaker. What is "heard" may have more to do with the hearer's preoccupations and presuppositions than with the speaker's intentions.

———————— ⟨⟨⟨⟩⟩⟩ ————————

Triple Think

I am well aware that James tells us that double-minded men tend to be unstable, but I am convinced that triple-thinking men have something going for them, particularly if they are preachers. W.E. Sangster wrote:

> The preacher will be that rarest of men—a *thinker*...After his devotions, the best hour of his day will be the hour given to sheer thinking: assembling the facts, facing their apparent contradiction, reaching for the help of God, and then, driving his brain like a bull-dozer through the apparent chaos...to order and understanding at the last."[2]

Perhaps the common use of the modern question, How do you feel about this? in place of the older, What do you think about this? is indicative of a significant trend.

―――――――― ⟨⟩ ――――――――

I'm not sure if by "apparent contradiction" he meant only difficulties in the text or if he was thinking of the difficulties that come from hearers who wish to contradict or question what the preacher says. My point is that preachers should think about what they say, what people think about what they say, and how to answer them in the sermon wherever possible. This is triple think, and it is a great way to clarify the message. Billy Graham has always used this method. He will make a statement. Then, putting into words what he assumes the people are thinking, he says, "But Billy, you say…" and then answers what they have "said" to Billy.

Define Your Terms

The old adage that "a picture is worth a thousand words" may be true, although some years ago in England the artistic establishment had egg on its collective face when it was discovered that the painting that had been adjudged the best example of modern art was the work of a three-year-old. Be that as it may, the question we need to ask is, If a picture is worth a thousand words, which words does it surpass in worth? And who decides? The answer, I suppose, is in the ear of the beholder. The problem with the preference for image over word is that it often betrays a preference for subjective ambiguity over objective precision.

Perhaps the common use of the modern question, How do you *feel* about this? in place of the older, What do you *think* about this? is indicative of a significant trend. This is something preachers should be aware of and should stand ready to address. If anything needs precision in communication, surely it is the timeless Word of God. This is

Preach It!

not to suggest that artistic portrayals of truth are inappropriate, but simply to underline the necessity of the careful use of words in the preaching of the Word. This requires at minimum careful definition, particularly as our culture is moving further and deeper into a wasteland of biblical illiteracy.

Often people think they know what you mean, and you assume they are tracking with you, but in my experience it is best to assume very little and to define terms thoroughly and often. I once asked a youth gathering, "Do you know what was written on the hypochondriac's epitaph?" They were silent, so I answered the question, "I told you I was sick!" Dead silence! It flew like the proverbial lead balloon, so I asked, "How many of you know what a hypochondriac is?" Not one knew. So I tried again. "How many know what an epitaph is?" Not one. That must have been close to the nadir of my communication career! Dare I ask, "How many of you know what a nadir is?"

When it comes to communication, definition is critical. If the preacher fears that this is too elementary and he is in danger of repeating basic truths ad nauseam, I would remind him of Dr. Johnson's dictum: "It is not adequately understood that men more often need to be reminded than instructed."

My observation is that many regular churchgoers would have difficulty defining *justification* or *born again* adequately. And not a few of them would greatly benefit from a definition of such taken-for-granted concepts as love and peace and joy—for the simple reason that the biblical understanding of these things varies dramatically from the common perceptions people so often bring to church with them.

———————— ⟨∽∾∾∽⟩ ————————

It is best to assume very little and to

define terms thoroughly and often.

clichés

I'm a little reluctant to use this example because it is extreme, but I think it will make an important point. Sometimes the way we quote Scripture must appear to some people to be a string of incomprehensible clichés. For instance, the well-loved "By grace you have been saved, through faith." What a superb truth—if you understand it—but what a confusing concept to a lot of people! Now that sounds heretical, but if we're going to communicate to people, they must hear what we say and they must understand what we mean by what we say. If they don't know what *saved* means and they don't know what *grace* is and they don't know what *faith* is, we can quote "By grace you have been saved, through faith" until we are blue in the face, and it won't do them any good.

To the young guy who is listening to you, the only idea of being saved he's ever had is to be pulled out of a river when drowning. The only Grace he knows is a blue-eyed blonde, and he distinctly remembers having a crush on a cheerleader in high school named Faith. She was a brown-eyed brunette. So while the preacher expounds Ephesians 2:8, the young man is thinking about being pulled out of a river by a blue-eyed blonde and a brown-eyed brunette. Now that's an extreme illustration, but not too extreme, as any preacher in touch with today's world knows.

The preacher must always assume there are listeners in the congregation who need to know, for instance, exactly what it means to be "washed in the blood of the Lamb"—because if they aren't told, they

---

Sometimes the way we quote Scripture must appear to some people to be a string of incomprehensible clichés.

might be excused for thinking that they have drifted into the company of very strange people who apparently engage in some very distasteful practices. The need for clarity and definition has always been there. The story is told of a printer who made a minor error when setting the type for a Bible. Although he got only one letter wrong, the minor error had major implications because his version read "Though I speak with the tongues of men and of angels, and have not *clarity*, I am become as sounding brass, or a tinkling cymbal." To have not clarity is serious!

The early Christians were accused of being incestuous because they married "brothers" or "sisters," they were accused of cannibalism because they "ate the flesh and drank the blood," and they were branded as atheists because they refused to worship the gods. To our minds these charges are ridiculous and blasphemous, but to people who did not understand what was going on, they were logically irrefutable. Explanation requires clarification, which includes definition.

Let Me Illustrate

How often I've seen the three little words "Let me illustrate," when inserted into a sermon, move like a breath of fresh air through a congregation! Ralph Waldo Emerson said, "I cannot hear a sermon without being struck by the fact that amid drowsy series of sentences what a sensation a historical fact, a biographical name, a sharply objective illustration makes."[3]

If illustrations served only to lighten the load of a "drowsy series of sentences," a good case could be made for using them, but illustrations play a much more significant role than that. Spurgeon started the section of his lectures titled "Illustrations in Preaching" by saying:

> The chief reason for the construction of windows in a house is...*to let in light*. Parables, similes, and metaphors have that effect; and hence we use them to *illustrate* our subject, or, in other words, to *"brighten with light,"* for that *is* Doctor Johnson's literal rendering of the word *illustrate*. Often when didactic speech fails to enlighten our hearers we may make them see our meaning by opening a window and letting in the pleasant light of analogy.[4]

So illustrations are windows letting in the pleasant light by which men and women "see" the message. But windows don't grow on trees. Windows need craftsmen and require work. And it is not easy work. Some time ago I was invited to team-teach a course called "Preaching From the Psalms" with Dr. Thomas Edward McComiskey at Trinity Evangelical Divinity School. Most of the students who enrolled in the class were graduates, and when I commented on this, they replied, "Here in seminary we learned our biblical languages, homiletics, and hermeneutics, but now we've been in the ministry for a little time, we realize we need help with illustration and application. We didn't learn how to do that."

With that in mind, I later asked Dr. Howard Hendricks, the master teacher from Dallas Seminary, "Can you teach 'illustrations'?" He replied that it is possible to teach the principles of illustrating but that learning to illustrate is primarily a matter of experience. But even experienced preachers still testify to the need to work at illustrating. John Stott, speaking about illustrations, confessed, "I know how bad I am at using them myself," but added, "I am trying to improve."[5] Despite the fact that his spoken and written illustrations are always compelling, his words are characteristically humble, and it's helpful for all preachers to know that a veteran preacher as gifted as John Stott is still trying to improve his sermon illustrations. We can all do that.

where to find them

But do I hear a mild complaint from an overworked preacher? Do I hear, "There you go. More work. When am I supposed to find the time to go around looking for sermon illustrations?" My response would be that while it requires work and will take time, you don't necessarily need to find a lot more time, because illustrations are happening around you all the time as you go about your daily tasks. Gathering illustrations has to do with living life with a great sense of curiosity. Preachers of earlier generations used illustrations which to us seem dated and often irrelevant (that is why many books of illustrations aren't always very helpful). They talked about kings long dead, steam engines and log cabins, and quiet moments reflecting on sunsets. They lived kinder and gentler and slower lives than we do. Our world is much faster paced and full of things to know. In their

Gathering illustrations has to do with
living life with a great sense of curiosity.

——————————— ⟨∘⁄∘⁄∘⟩ ———————————

book *Inductive Preaching,* Ralph L. Lewis and Gregg Lewis inform us that "the Huntsville Computer Center claims that the fund of information making up human knowledge has doubled on the average of once every two years since 1960. It's now doubling every six months."[6]

The problem is not that there are too few illustrations but that our eyes are not sufficiently open to see them. The preacher should be a student of life as it passes by. Wherever the preacher lives and moves, there the world is full of illustrations. Something is always happening. Somebody is always doing something, saying something. Stories are told, fears revealed, excitement generated, facts accumulated, aspirations born. All this is going on as we move among people. Birds fly, squirrels squirrel, ice freezes, clouds scud, fishermen fish, sunbeams dance, dogs sniff. Incidentally, all this is going on outside my study window as I write on a bitterly cold February day.

Reading through *The Quotable Spurgeon,* I was particularly impressed to find that in each memorable selection from his preaching there was at least one illustration, each of which was remarkably homely. For instance, he talked about stones on the seashore, insects, flowers, and bees in a hive. Of course, he had an excellent model in the Master Illustrator himself, of whom Tyrell Green wrote:

> He spoke of lilies, vines and corn,
> The sparrow and the raven;
> And words so natural, yet so wise
> Were on men's hearts engraven.
> And yeast and bread, and flax and cloth,
> And eggs and fish and candles
> See how the most familiar world
> He most divinely handles.[7]

At the same time, all kinds of different things are happening to people in the congregation. People in my church love to be asked to keep me supplied with interesting anecdotes, quotations, and personal experiences. So my mail regularly includes clippings from the Wall Street Journal, movie reviews, book reports, and the like, and my elbow is often tugged by someone saying, "Stuart, did you hear about such and such?" In fact, involving people in the process of illustration and application not only enriches the preacher's communication, but it also stimulates people's listening, because they don't want to miss "their" illustrations—and they want to make sure I relate them correctly.

powers of observation

I learned the necessity of developing powers of observation after reading Harold Fuller's book *Run While the Sun Is Hot.* In it he tells the story of a tour of ministry he took in the sub-Sahara. It is full of the kind of vivid, descriptive detail that would escape the drowsy traveler but that enlivens the experience of those who have eyes to see. Some years after reading the book, my wife and I traveled through the same region. One day in Benin, in the middle of nowhere, I got into a conversation with an Australian missionary. I commented that I was surprised to see so many birds in such a parched, barren place.

He promptly started to talk with great enthusiasm and expertise on the varieties of indigenous birds. I asked how they survived. So he explained how the artesian water supply works under the desert, producing vegetation to support insect life and plant life, which in turn makes it possible for birds to flourish. In response to my further questioning, he explained the

---

People in my church love to be asked to keep me supplied with interesting anecdotes, quotations, and personal experiences.

connection between the artesian water and the unique rock formations and flora and fauna in the area. The conversation went on for a long time as the missionary demonstrated a fascinating wealth of knowledge of the environment in which he lived, an environment in which, at first sight, nothing much was happening but which to the eye of the curious observer was full of delight. And for the preacher, it was replete with illustrations.

I came away convinced that if the desert is full of such wonder to the eager eye, there is no excuse for the preacher who fails to live vitally aware of the surrounding world, full as it is of interesting data that cry out to be used as bridges over which the truth can pass into the inner recesses of human hearts.

storerooms for illustrations

Jesus said a teacher "is like the owner of a house who brings out of his storeroom new treasures as well as old" (Matthew 13:52). The modern preacher's storeroom may be a filing cabinet stuffed with clippings, a notebook full of scribbled notes, a Rolodex of neatly typed information, or a computer with a readily accessible database of information. Or it may be all of the above. But the preacher should have a storeroom, and he should bring new things out of it rather than relying on threadbare stories that the congregation can tell as well as he.

some illustrations of illustrating

An illustration may be nothing more than a striking simile. I once heard a preacher say that the members of his congregation looked like "hooting owls sitting on tombstones." Descriptive if not complimentary or judicious, but certainly striking! Or an illustration can be a succinct phrase. On one occasion I talked to approximately a hundred college students about priorities, and I challenged them to discover if their top priority was the kingdom of God (as per Matthew 6:33) or the empire of self. The phrase "the empire of self" stuck in the minds of a number of students who talked to me about it afterward.

An illustration may be a relevant quotation that makes a point better than you can. I can't come close to G.K. Chesterton's definition of *tradition*, so why use mine when I can use his? "Tradition may be

There is no excuse for the preacher who fails to live vitally aware of the surrounding world.

⎯⎯⎯⎯⎯ ⟡ ⎯⎯⎯⎯⎯

defined as an extension of the franchise. Tradition means giving votes to the most obscure of all classes, our ancestors. It is the democracy of the dead."[8] Or a quotation may add credibility to your statement because of the stature of the person quoted. So I can offer my opinions about the condition of American society and the pressing need for a recovery of biblical truth, but Robert Bellah's conclusions in his best-selling *Habits of the Heart* will carry much more weight: "Our society has been deeply influenced by the tradition of modern individualism. We have taken the position that our most important task today is the recovery of the insights of the older biblical and republican traditions."[9] Then again, the poignancy of a quotation may be directly related to the condition of the person being quoted. I vividly remember an annual church meeting when a four-year-old girl was interviewed on camera. When she was asked, "What do you like most about God?" she replied with utter simplicity and winsomeness, "I like being able to dream about him at night." A quotation like that will wing its way into many a heart. An expression like the one I have just used, "wing its way," with its suggestive pictorial character, will help fix the idea of truth being assimilated much better than just saying, "An illustration can help you remember something."

Because I have already mentioned the value of storytelling, I won't say more on that subject, but obviously good, interesting, relevant stories do wonders for a sermon and more than wonders for the hearers. And not just in terms of clarification! A well-placed anecdote can refresh and renew a congregation and help people settle down for further teaching at a time when they might have come to the conclusion that enough was enough. George A. Buttrick said, "It is often wise to allow a congregation to sit down awhile on a milestone and rest. A judiciously placed and

*Good, interesting, relevant stories do
wonders for a sermon and more than
wonders for the hearers.*

———— ⚬⁄⚬⁄⚬⁆ ————

chosen illustration will serve that purpose."[10] I might add that the further the milestone is from the beginning of the sermon and the longer the journey, the more appreciated the rest will be.

It is also worth noting that illustrations can be singularly effective if incorporated at the beginning and the end of a sermon. In the first instance they capture attention, as we have already discussed, and in the latter they help to nail down the truth that's been preached, to summarize what's been taught, and to send people on their way with something upon which to hang their thoughts.

To be effective, illustrations should be intelligible, intriguing, illuminating, and inviting. I once heard a man trying to illustrate the work of the church by using the analogy of the operations of a business with which he was acquainted. He launched into a description of how raw materials were collected, the chemical processes to which they were subjected, the ways in which the various side products were utilized, how the main product was tested and evaluated, and the marketing techniques the company had developed. All this information would, no doubt, have been extremely interesting to people in that business, but it was nearly incomprehensible to those of us who had no knowledge of the business and even less desire to learn about it.

The result was that what had been reasonably clear in the first place (that is, how the church works) was actually obscured by an illustration that was supposed to make it more intelligible. Phillips Brooks said it well: "Some preachers tow all great subjects out to sea and then escape in small boats through the fog."[11] The small boats used by some preachers are leaky illustrations. I have been guilty of this myself, as was brought home to me one day when I gave an illustration about a hair-raising plane journey that I thought made the point perfectly clear. Unfortunately, my listeners were so worried about how I survived—which I omitted from the account—that they totally missed the point!

тhe "so-whαт" нυмρ

When mountain climbing in the beautiful Lake District of England where I grew up, I often had the experience of climbing up to what appeared to be the summit, only to discover that the real pinnacle was still ahead. It was impossible to reach the top without first negotiating the brow of the intervening spur. There is in every sermon at least one spur on the way to the summit. I call it the so-what hump. The preacher who is wrapped up in the wonder of the truth, which he has been studying all week but to which his listeners have come in cold, may overlook the fact that the people sitting out there are wondering, "So what?" They are thinking, "What in the world is the point of all this information that is flowing unchecked like a torrent from the lips of our preacher this morning? He is obviously transported with delight; but I am sitting here mildly bemused by his erudition, confused as to the point, and amused by his enthusiasm over such irrelevancies." These people are in danger of being left halfway up the mountain because the preacher has not helped them over the so-what hump.

My wife has often pointed out to me that I have a tendency to leave people to negotiate the hump on their own. The reason for this is that I tend to think in terms of principles that I feel reasonably confident I can apply to specific situations. But my wife insists that many people do not think as I do, and they want to be shown exactly what to do in specific situations. I have to admit I fear insulting people's intelligence by telling them how a certain principle applies, and I am nervous about adding my own application to eternal truth—an application that is relevant to me but is not necessarily universally relevant. So I have tended to back off. I believe deeply that the preacher's job is to preach the truth in general, and the Holy Spirit's role is to make it truth in particular. But even with all these caveats, I still think my wife is right, because she is a skilled and gifted communicator herself and I have seen her effectiveness in applying the truth. The question then becomes, At what point in the sermon should application be made? The answer will be determined to some extent by the style of message being preached. In some instances, for example in inductive or certain types of narrative preaching, the application will often come at the end. But in other instances, it is helpful if the application is made during the sermon.

The preacher's job is to preach the truth

in general, and the Holy Spirit's role

is to make it truth in particular.

Recently I preached from John 15:18–16:4. It was necessary to explain exactly what John meant by "the world" that hated Jesus and would hate his disciples. And it was clear to me that people would need to understand why it might hate them. But I knew that some people might not have any idea that the antagonism they were encountering as new Christians was directly related to their testimonies and the antipathy of some people to their beliefs.

So I gave the example of a wife who as a pagan had married another pagan so they might have a delightfully middle-class American pagan marriage. After a while she became disillusioned with her marriage and talked to her friend about it. She discovered that her friend had "gotten religion." Being eager to get help wherever it might be found, she went along with her friend to a seminar, which led eventually to her becoming a Christian. Her husband then became increasingly irritated by what was happening in her life, for the simple reason that he was now, for all practical purposes, living with a woman whom he had not married. His disappointment, his sense of betrayal, his anger at his wife for changing the rules halfway through the game became centered on the church and

Christ, and he began to hate them both. This led to abusive language and increasingly abusive behavior so that the marriage became unbearable.

Many people in the congregation readily understood the application. It helped them to understand what was going on in their lives and led them to a point where they were ready to see that the rest of the passage dealing with the promised Holy Spirit was wonderfully relevant to them in their difficult marital situations. A little later in the message, it was necessary to show how tensions may arise in the workplace when people develop a different work ethic after coming to Christ, and how these tensions can lead to deep problems with union officials and workmates. And as there were many young students in attendance, it was appropriate to explain what would happen to them if their adherence to Christian ethics affected the grading curve for the whole class, a situation not designed to add to their popularity with the rest of the student body but necessary if they were to be disciples of Christ. As a result of these illustrative applications, I later had serious conversations with students, Christian spouses, and workers.

Ian MacPherson states well the need for illustration and application:

> The message we are called upon to deliver is in some senses deep and dark and difficult…In it there are depths that the profoundest intellect cannot plumb…To grapple with such great and glorious realities is a task far beyond our finite human reason…If we are to present them intelligently we shall have to interpret the spiritual by the natural, the unknown by the known, the abstract by the concrete, the general by the particular. In other words we shall have to illustrate.[12]

Much more could be said on the subject, but if you wish to study it further let me recommend Spurgeon's chapter "Illustrations in Preaching" in his *Lectures to My Students,* the whole of Part 2 of Sangster's book *The Craft of the Sermon,* and the chapter titled "Examples and Illustrations" in David Buttrick's comprehensive book *Homiletic.*

> *"Some preachers tow all great subjects*
> *out to sea and then escape in small*
> *boats through the fog."*

---————————— ◄⊙⁄⊙► —————————---

Endnotes

1. Deborah Tannen, *You Just Don't Understand* (New York: Ballantine Books, 1990), 13.

2. W.E. Sangster, *The Craft of the Sermon* (London: Epworth Press, 1954), 150.

3. Sangster, *The Craft of the Sermon,* 200.

4. Charles H. Spurgeon, *Lectures to My Students* (London: Marshall Pickering, first published 1954, reissued 1989), 349.

5. John R.W. Stott, *Between Two Worlds* (Grand Rapids, Mich.: Wm. B. Eerdmans, 1982), 236.

6. Ralph L. Lewis and Gregg Lewis, *Inductive Preaching* (Westchester, Ill.: Crossway Books, 1983), 27.

7. Ian MacPherson, *The Art of Illustrating Sermons* (New York: Abingdon Press, 1964), 40.

8. George J. Marlin, ed., *The Quotable Chesterton* (San Francisco: Ignatius Press, 1986), 351.

9. Robert N. Bellah, *Habits of the Heart* (New York: Harper and Row, 1986), 303.

10. MacPherson, *The Art of Illustrating Sermons,* 28.

11. Craig Skinner, *The Teaching Ministry of the Pulpit* (Grand Rapids, Mich.: Baker Books, 1973), 173.

12. MacPherson, *The Art of Illustrating Sermons,* 15.

chapter 15

Crafting Conclusions

A number of years ago, I was invited to speak at Peninsula Bible Church in Palo Alto, California. The senior pastor, my dear friend the late Ray Stedman, introduced me with typical humor. "Friends," he said, "Stuart's here again. I guess I should say something about him, but I don't know what to say." He paused and then continued with a twinkle in his eye, "Oh, yes! There's one thing you probably don't know about Stuart Briscoe, but he is the man of whom Billy Graham once said, 'Who?' " The audience laughed, and I spoke.

Some time later Ray was a guest in our home, and as I introduced him to my younger son, Pete, who was probably thirteen at the time, I related the above story. To my surprise, Pete did not laugh, even though he has a great sense of humor. He turned to Ray and said, "Dr. Stedman, you think you know my father, but it is obvious you don't. Because anyone who knows my father knows that he needs no introduction, but he sure needs a conclusion!" (My reputation for needing a conclusion goes back to the first sermon I ever preached, as you may remember from Chapter 1.)

Some sermons are like golf balls, which often continue to roll after they should have stopped. Perhaps preachers who suffer from that tendency take comfort from the fact that in his letter to the Philippians, Paul wrote *finally* well before he finished! He could have said "lastly" and then lasted! The apostle's example notwithstanding, it is good for a sermon to arrive at a conclusion in a timely fashion. A sermon that

> *"Anyone who knows my father knows that he needs no introduction, but he sure needs a conclusion!"*

has difficulty stopping can quickly undo any good it achieved while it was moving along. Preachers who go on after they've finished will quickly irritate their hearers if the hearers suspect that the preachers don't know how to wind it all up because they haven't prepared for the final moment. Listeners will quickly resent being required to be spectators of a work in progress while the line at the restaurant grows ever longer. But far more importantly, the congregation should leave the sermon with minds and hearts full of information rather than of irritation. The way the preacher concludes the sermon will have much to do with the way people leave and what they carry away with them. The conclusion of a sermon should have similarities to the way in which items purchased at a supermarket are packaged and delivered to the car. In both cases everything is neatly accounted for, put in place, and presented in manageable form, ready to be taken home.

An effective sermon will have addressed the whole person. Mind, will, and emotions will have felt the impact of the preaching of the Word. The conclusion should briefly, and I emphasize *briefly*, summarize the salient points that should have made an impact on the mind during the course of the preaching. The emotional and motivational force of the information that has been intellectually appropriated should be underlined, if possible, by an illustration, and the challenge to obedience or dependence that the preaching will have prompted should be made abundantly clear. Preaching that incorporates all three dimensions is likely, under the Spirit's operation, to produce a response.

Preachers must studiously avoid manipulating a response that may subsequently abort. Undue challenges without adequate explanations are a case in point. Wills pushed to respond to truth that minds have not grasped and assimilated rarely produce fruits of righteousness. Emotions played upon by polished motivators, before the Spirit has had time to take the truth home to the heart, will dive as promptly to disillusionment as they leaped to response. At the same time, preaching that lays out truth in a flat, unemotional, unchallenging manner can hardly be mistaken for the truth of the Bible which gladdens the heart, feeds the mind, challenges the will, and changes lives. All this to show that the conclusion is more important than we may have been led to believe.

I believe that sermons usually should be ended with prayer. When I lead the congregation in prayer at the end of a sermon, I generally introduce it by saying something like this: "We're now going to pray, and it may be that you wish to respond to the Lord in your own heart. But you may not be sure how to phrase what you want to say or how to express what you're feeling. My prayer could be your prayer. If you find it matches what is going on in your heart at this time, make it your own. You don't need to say it out loud. God is not hard of hearing." The prayer is then a simple summary of the things one could reasonably expect people would want to say to the Lord. I find that these few moments at the end of a sermon are usually deeply significant. A stillness settles over the congregation as men and women talk to the Lord after they've given careful attention to what he had to say to them.

In some traditions a more formalized "invitation" is extended at the end of a service. In a large auditorium or stadium, this gives opportunity for follow-up to those who may respond to an evangelistic message but would not be reached any other way. In regular church services the situation is different, but the invitation can be helpful. It may give an opportunity to those who wish to make an external demonstration of

The congregation should leave the sermon with minds and hearts full of information rather than of irritation.

their response to the Word to do so. The way they do this may take different forms. Raising a hand, standing in place, walking down the aisle, or kneeling at a Communion rail are all common examples. There is no doubt that this type of activity can solidify for some people the action they take in their hearts. It also can lead people to a confession of their faith, although it can become a substitute for confession with the mouth (or a clearly articulated statement of faith), which Paul shows is a means of other people hearing the Word and coming to faith (see Romans 10:9-14).

We offer a variety of opportunities for people to respond if they wish.

I try to bear in mind that I'm preaching to a wide variety of people and that it's very easy for some of them to be put off—or utterly confused—by a certain concluding approach to the sermon. Accordingly, we offer a variety of opportunities for people to respond if they wish. We point out that there are pastors standing at the front of the sanctuary if they wish to talk to a pastor. On the other hand, we tell people we have a room off the sanctuary called the Quiet Corner, where those who prefer that approach may go to pray or talk in peaceful surroundings and find help from a layperson. This way we offer something for those who don't mind coming up to the front…and something for those who would find that experience to be totally intimidating. There is something for those who will talk only to a pastor and something for those who would run a mile rather than talk to a pastor. Some people don't want to go anywhere, front or back, and they don't want to talk to anybody, pastor or layperson, but they *do* want help. So for them we have cards in the pews on which they can state whatever it is they want us to know, and they can either hand them in at the information center or mail them when they get home and have had time to think about it a little more. We guide those who have more mundane questions to the information stations. This way we don't pressure people into a response that they might not be ready for and that could be counterproductive, but at the same time we don't make it easy for people to disregard the importance of the Word and the necessity for them to respond.

As I mentioned earlier, the Points to Ponder, which are part of the outline distributed to all members of the congregation, serve as a provocative concluding summary and response so everybody is confronted with stimulants to thought and action—which is exactly what we hope the preaching will achieve.

Emotions played upon by polished motivators, before the Spirit has had time to take the truth home to the heart, will dive as promptly to disillusionment as they leaped to response.

part 4
Time to Let Yourself Go

chapter 16

Being a Free and Joyful Preacher

You remember my farmer friends who encouraged me in the early days? They had never heard of Dr. Denney (neither had I in those days), but they would have sympathized with his sentiments: "The man who shoots above the target does not thereby prove he has superior ammunition. He simply proves that he is not an accurate shot."[1] And they would have been delighted with the answer of one of their lay pastors who, when he was asked about how he prepared for preaching, said:

> First I reads meself full,
> Then I thinks meself clear,
> Then I prays meself hot,
> Then I lets meself go.

So far we have been considering what "reads meself full" and "thinks meself clear" and "prays meself hot" mean, and it remains only for us to look into what it means to "let meself go." Or to change the analogy to bring it into line with what we have been considering: what it means to stand in the full blessing of personal and technical preparation before pews full of people invigorated through a vital worship experience and ready to hear from the Word. One could reasonably expect a fullness of joy for preacher and hearer alike.

what to expect

What does this mean for the preacher and the congregation? What can the preacher realistically expect, and what are the people in the congregation likely to experience if there has been careful preparation such as we have tried to outline? The preacher should be able to stand before the people with a marked degree of confidence that the Lord is going to speak to them. By the same token, the people should anticipate they will hear something from the Lord that will be relevant to their lives. Now I am aware that those sentiments sound ominously like clichés, but if we are to take preaching seriously and if we are to conduct ourselves correctly in the preaching task, these are not clichés. They are powerful realities. I submit to you that the prepared preacher and the expectant people together create an environment in which the proclamation of eternal truth is much more than a routine affair.

How far removed from "routine" can the preaching be expected to roam? We may not be free to expect in the ordinary scheme of events the extraordinary dramatic signs that sometimes followed the preaching of the great revivals (although there is no reason to believe those days are gone forever). Extraordinary events, by definition, do not happen ordinarily. We may not see whole towns converted, sinners falling down and confessing their sins in the streets, and so forth, but it is perfectly appropriate for modern-day preachers and congregations to expect lives to be touched, marriages saved, families restored, addicts released, and sinners both respectable and reprobate to be regenerated, renewed, and

It is perfectly appropriate for modern-day preachers and congregations to expect lives to be touched, marriages saved, families restored, addicts released, and sinners both respectable and reprobate to be regenerated, renewed, and redeemed.

redeemed. These evidences, which for some preachers have become extraordinary, could realistically be expected as normative responses to the preaching of the Word. Strange as it may seem, these occurrences are remarkably rare in many churches. But even stranger, many of these churches have long since settled into a posture where very little is expected, and so they are rarely surprised by anything happening. As the old adage reminds us, "Blessed is he that expecteth nothing, for he shall not be disappointed."

confidence and expectancy

The preacher, therefore, should be prepared to speak with great confidence and expectancy. This confidence is far removed from self-confidence, of course. It is confidence rooted in the promise that the Word does not "return void," and it is confidence predicated on the fact that the same Holy Spirit who inspired the Word broods over the gathering, anoints the preacher to interpret the Word, indwells believers, and graciously ministers to unbelievers in order to implement the Word. It is, moreover, confidence that stems from knowing that preaching is divinely ordained and that preachers are people to whom God has given the "best and happiest" thing to do. The preacher who knows and deeply believes these facts is a confident, expectant preacher.

The preacher should be prepared to speak with great confidence and expectancy.

comfortable and natural

Confident preachers are much more likely to say, "I lets meself go" than are those who feel either technically ill-prepared or spiritually out of touch. Or both. And what do these confident preachers look like? They look comfortable and natural when they stand to preach, like well-trained and carefully prepared athletes whose apparent ease of performance

Their highly visible gifting does not make them superior any more than noses are superior to hearts because of their prominence.

disguises an assiduous commitment to sacrifice and training. They are comfortable with their calling because they know it is of God and not of themselves. They did not choose to preach. They know that for reasons known only to God they were chosen to preach. They stumbled on this glorious discovery when they were helped to identify gifts and aspirations that could have come only from the Spirit of God. They have a heart for the people of God, a desire for the glory of God, a hunger for the Word of God, a dependence on the Spirit of God, a love for the Son of God, and a burden for those without the knowledge of God.

These preachers are comfortable with being gifted because the very term *gift* presupposes *giver*. They know the Spirit distributes the gifts as he chooses, and he apparently chose them. They have long since come to terms with the fact that this does not make them superior because of their highly visible gifting any more than noses are superior to hearts because of their prominence. Granted, their special gift carries special responsibilities, but they have humbly come to terms with these, too, and have learned to accept the challenge of being accountable, because they have also accepted the special enabling that God supplies with every calling. They know that *they* cannot save a single soul, open a solitary blind eye, or turn anyone from darkness to light or from the power of Satan to God. But they also know that *God* can and still does and that he uses people just like them as his agents. And they are ecstatic about being in the loop.

They see themselves as being in the same line (if not the same league) as Augustine and Chrysostom, Luther and Calvin, Wesley and Whitfield,

Lloyd-Jones and Graham. They have gifts that differ, but they preach the same gospel. Their circumstances differ but not their calling. The personalities are different, but they have preaching in common. Their attitudes differ, but their aim is unerringly the same. They are all links in one gloriously long chain of men and women who will continue to proclaim the truth until preaching is no longer necessary, for the kingdom finally will have come. As they stand before the people, they know their own sinfulness, but they have dealt with it. They know forgiveness and have appropriated it. They are excruciatingly aware of their inadequacy, but in the Spirit they have learned to cope with it. No one need remind them of their unworthiness, for they have just talked to the Lord about it, and he told them it wasn't a problem, as he specializes in using such people because they are the only kind available. So they are comfortable people.

free and fresh

Phillips Brooks told this to the students of Yale Divinity School:

> Truth through personality is our description of real preaching. The truth must really come through the person, not merely over his lips, not merely into his understanding and out through his pen. It must come through his character, his affections, his whole intellectual and moral being. It must come genuinely through him...with all the earnestness and strength in him.[2]

Brooks' concern, as I understand it, was not only that the preacher should be captivated and molded by the truth preached, but that the result should be "a broad, free, fresh meeting of a man with men, in such close contact that the Christ who has entered into his life may, through his, enter into theirs."[3] The words *broad, free,* and *fresh* are significant because they speak of the individual uniqueness of the preacher. They describe the personality through which the truth will be channeled. But it is at this very point that some preachers come unglued, for they are not free and fresh enough to be comfortable being themselves.

As soon as some preachers stand before the people, they are changed into other people. The moment they open their mouths, a stranger speaks. They would never talk to their families or friends the way they talk in the pulpit. But for some reason, they feel it necessary to put on a tone of voice that would sound ludicrous elsewhere, and they adopt mannerisms that would be decidedly odd outside the pulpit. Maybe they had a beloved homiletics professor from a different era who did it this way, and they either were given or gained the impression that this was the only way to do it. Or perhaps they saw a television evangelist drawing big crowds and decided that this methodology might work for them. When I was a young man, Billy Graham came to Harringay Arena in London and wowed the evangelical wing of the British church. In no time at all, most of us young preachers were holding our Bibles draped over our left hands, stabbing the air with the forefingers of our right hands, and pronouncing with great gusto, "The Bible says…" with a North Carolina accent, no less! But while we admired the way in which the truth was being communicated through Graham's personality, by no stretch of the imagination could it be said that the truth was being communicated through our personalities. So we were neither free nor fresh.

Know Thyself

My wife and I are quite different in our approaches to preaching. Jill prepares meticulously, making copious notes with various colored pens and all manner of lines and stars and cute little symbols that mean something only to her. She needs to know exactly what she is going to say and makes sure she does know before she starts. She expounds the Scriptures well and loves, as she explains it, "to peek around the corner of the verse." By that she means she likes to ask questions such as "Did Mrs. Noah like animals?" She certainly captures people's attention by such an approach and ingeniously draws out spiritual truths from such unpromising sources. She uses humor almost invariably aimed at herself and speaks openly about her own failures and frailties, which means she enjoys great empathy with and from the people.

My approach is quite different. I speak from my skeleton outline, and I have enough material in my head for at least two sermons. As the sermon progresses, I try to sense the mood of the congregation and

As I preach, I adjust. The result is that

although I preach the same sermon in

all four of our weekend services,

each version is quite different.

───────── ⌒∞∞⌒ ─────────

select the material in my head that I think will be most appropriate. So as I preach, I adjust. The result is that although I preach the same sermon in all four of our weekend services, each version is quite different. I, too, use humor but of a totally different kind from Jill's. (I don't care if Mrs. Noah liked animals, but I like to tell people that her name was Joan of Ark.) I don't often talk about my own failures, not because I don't have any but because I'm not particularly comfortable talking about myself that way and I can't imagine why anybody would want to know anyway. What Jill calls "peeking around the corner of the verse" in my book sometimes looks suspiciously like "wandering up the other end of the block." But I never did see myself as being half as creative and imaginative as she is.

My point in boring you with the differences in our approaches is to illustrate how we have learned to be free and fresh in terms of our unique personalities. Neither of us feels under any pressure to imitate the other, although both of us gladly testify to having learned from each other. As I've listened to Jill talking about her own fears, I've recognized the very real response from the congregation, and I've learned how to share more of myself in my preaching. I don't feel compelled to say what I don't want to say, but at the same time, I've realized the necessity to overcome my own shyness and reluctance in order to enhance the communication of the truth. In the same way, as I sometimes talk to Jill about what seems to me to be her overly exuberant piece of "creativity" that may border on the fanciful, she has always been eager to make the necessary adjustments to her approach without losing her unique ability to make the Scriptures live for people.

Humor

I mentioned that both Jill and I use humor in our preaching, although our senses of humor are different. This is because our personalities are different. It would not be very natural for me to poke fun at myself as Jill does at herself, and Jill often has problems relating the kind of humorous stories that I like to use. She has a tendency to start with the punch line and work toward the beginning, which is as endearing as it is confusing. As Phillips Brooks reminds us, it is a matter of truth through personality.

This brings us to an important consideration with regard to humor in preaching. If the preacher's personality plays a significant role in the communication of truth, as Brooks insists it does, and if the preacher has a keen sense of humor, then it would be strange if the humor were not a powerful weapon in his or her armory. But not all preachers are enthusiastic about the use of humor in the pulpit. Dr. Martyn Lloyd-Jones wrote:

> I would not dare to say that there is no place for humor in preaching; but I do suggest that it is not a very big place because of the nature of the work, and because of the character of the Truth with which it is dealing…The most one can say for the place of humor is that it is only allowable if it is natural. The man who tries to be humorous is an abomination and should never be allowed to enter a pulpit.[4]

There can be little doubt that the doctor was right to express concern, if he was referring to the kind of humor that trivializes the deep doctrines of the faith and serves either to manipulate the congregation or to enhance its view of the preacher's likability. But even he conceded (reluctantly?) that it was permissible if natural. David Buttrick seems to take a more positive view while sounding a similar and appropriate word of caution. Concerning "humorous illustrations," he wrote, "We can state a general rule with ease: If you are a naturally funny person, your problem will be control; if you are not a naturally funny person, do not try."[5]

It is a matter of truth through personality.

—————————— ⌒⌒⌒ ——————————

Perhaps another way of looking at it would be to ask if what is called "natural" is actually a gift from the Lord to be used appropriately. Malcolm Muggeridge certainly thought so. I remember hearing him speak in Lausanne, Switzerland, and his use of humor was brilliant. He delighted to tell how on one occasion he was looking at the soaring spire of Salisbury Cathedral and following its elegant lines up into the heavens. His spirit was lifted, his thoughts turned heavenward because, as he explained, "spires are meant to inspire." But then he noticed under the edges of the roof the grinning faces of the gargoyles, reminding him that from earth's vantage point, man's heavenly aspirations often appear superb, but from heaven's perspective they are slightly ludicrous. His point was that humor, like spires and gargoyles, is "an expression, in terms of the grotesque, of the inexorable disparity between human aspiration and human performance."[6] If humor is an expression of the disparity between human aspiration and human performance, it is easy to see that it can be a tremendous tool for communicating a message that is concerned not only to point out that disparity in unmistakable terms, but also to point unerringly to the gospel that takes man from where he is to where God wants him to be. The gospel is designed for the banishing of the "inexorable disparity" and the bridging of the great gulf between aspiration and performance.

Much more could be said on the subject, but Phillips Brooks shall have the last word, for now. He told the students at Yale:

> Humor involves the perception of the true proportions of life. It is one of the most helpful qualities that the preacher can possess. There is no extravagance which deforms the pulpit which would not be modified and repressed, often entirely obliterated, if the minister had a true sense of humor. It has softened the bitterness of controversy a thousand times. You cannot encourage it too much.

He also recommended that preachers should read the humorous works of the great authors, which, he said, "will help you to keep from extravagances without fading into insipidity. They will preserve your gravity while they save you from pompous solemnity."[7]

So the task of preachers is not an easy one. They must not fail to take seriously the burden of preaching eternal truth to finite people, knowing full well the incalculable consequences of response, or lack of it, to the Word preached. If they present the truth with levity, it will hardly be accepted with gravity. But if the solemnity of the task appears to the listeners to be so oppressive that the preacher no longer resembles an ordinary person, the truth will hardly be welcomed enthusiastically by ordinary people. Preachers must always ask with the apostle, "Who is sufficient for these things?" knowing full well they are not. In concert with Paul, preachers must always answer the question with great joy, "Our sufficiency is of God." It is this understanding that allows preachers on the one hand to preach, in Baxter's words, "as a dying man to dying men" and yet on the other hand to do it with such relaxed freedom and delight that the message comes across powerfully and attractively.

Endnotes

1. Ian MacPherson, *The Art of Illustrating Sermons* (New York: Abingdon Press, 1964), 129.

2. Phillips Brooks, *The Joy of Preaching* (Grand Rapids, Mich.: Kregel Publications, 1989), 27.

3. Brooks, *The Joy of Preaching*, 88.

4. D. Martyn Lloyd-Jones, *Preaching and Preachers* (London: Hodder and Stoughton, 1971), 241.

5. David Buttrick, *Homiletic* (Philadelphia: Fortress Press, 1987), 146.

6. John R.W. Stott, *Between Two Worlds* (Grand Rapids, Mich.: Wm. B. Eerdmans, 1982), 291.

7. Brooks, *The Joy of Preaching*, 58.

chapter ⑰

······································

Speaking With Freedom

Dr. Martyn Lloyd-Jones agreed with Phillips Brooks about truth being communicated through personality and added:

> In preaching, all one's faculties should be engaged, the whole man should be involved. I go so far as to suggest that even the body should be involved.[1]

The idea of the body being involved may seem a little odd, but the correct and judicious use of action in preaching can make all the difference between a sermon that either grips people or leaves them quietly to dream the hour away. Dr. Lloyd-Jones reminds us that the great Demosthenes, when asked about the first, second, and third *desiderata* of rhetoric, replied, "Action, action, action." Obviously some preachers are more free than others, both in their personalities and in their preaching styles. The preacher reading from a manuscript will probably make minimal use of the body as a means of communicating the message. The head will be bowed most of the time, with an occasional glance at the congregation (perhaps to assure himself that they are still there). There may be an occasional movement of an arm or two to reinforce a point, but there will be no departure from the pulpit itself. This being the case, the preacher is asking much more of the congregation's powers of concentration than the one who incorporates action that holds attention and emphasizes the spoken word. This is particularly relevant in a visually oriented culture in which people's attention spans

The correct and judicious use of action in preaching can make all the difference between a sermon that either grips people or leaves them quietly to dream the hour away.

———————— ✺ ————————

have been ruined by too much passive watching of television, where there is either dramatic action or constantly changing camera angles. People have become used to action.

In some churches, of course, the possibilities of action are severely curtailed by the architecture of the building, and in particular the pulpit itself. Spurgeon had some choice words to say on the subject of pulpits. He grumbled:

> What horrible inventions they are!…Remarkable are the forms which pulpits have assumed according to the freaks of human fancy and folly…What could have been their design and intent it would be hard to conjecture. A deep wooden pulpit of the old sort might well remind a minister of his mortality, for it is nothing but a coffin set on end: But on what rational ground do we bury our pastors alive?[2]

Some preachers who have been sentenced to be locked up in old-fashioned pulpits have managed to inject action into their preaching despite the obvious disadvantages of their confinement. One cleric was waving his arms vigorously as he eloquently and enthusiastically preached his sermon. A small boy sitting on the front row, mesmerized by the performance, whispered to his mother, "Mommy, what happens if that man gets out?" No doubt in his youthful mind he wondered why anyone would allow himself to be voluntarily cooped up in such a confined space—a question that may have crossed many a preacher's mind, too.

Let's assume for the moment that we are not confined to an action-inhibiting pulpit. What advantages are there if a preacher is free and fresh and it shows in energetic action? The words to describe such action are *mobility, flexibility, proximity,* and *vitality.*

A moment's reflection will show that all these words are singularly attractive and when applied to preaching can help make the communication of truth much more effective.

Mobility

Dr. Ben Haden of First Presbyterian Church, Chattanooga, Tennessee, is a good example of a preacher who holds attention by being mobile as he preaches. His legal background is still in the foreground in the way he dispenses with a pulpit and presents his sermons in the manner of a trial attorney addressing a jury. This is an excellent way of compelling people to be involved in the proceedings.

The church in which I minister has a worship center where people are seated through about 250 degrees. This means, of course, that a considerable number of people are actually seated behind the pulpit, so I am careful to move around on an open platform to address them. Some time ago one of the Milwaukee papers devoted the front cover and a large segment of the Sunday supplement to a story about the ministry of Elmbrook Church. The paper laid quite an emphasis on my style of preaching, illustrating it with "action" pictures, all of which, the paper stated, were taken within a sixty-second time slot. It almost made me dizzy to look at them, but from the purely dispassionate perspective

---

Dr. Ben Haden dispenses with a pulpit and presents his sermons in the manner of a trial attorney addressing a jury.

of the secular press (if the press has one) there was something interesting about this approach.

I have received similar responses from people who watch me preaching on television, although one lady did write in to say that I remind her of a caged tiger. She didn't state any particular aversion to either caged tigers or animated preachers, though, and I much prefer being compared to a tiger than to a *Cholopus Didactylus*—a sloth.

Being mobile is particularly helpful, or perhaps even necessary, when a narrative style sermon is being presented. To convey the full intent and drama of the story may well require a certain amount of "acting out." One Easter Sunday I decided to tell the Easter story from the point of view of the two disciples bound for Emmaus. A significant part of the dialogue of the story (amplified to explain it for the benefit of our regular three-times-a-year attenders who have no idea where Emmaus is, or if it is a state of mind) took place as they were walking along. It would have seemed rather odd to tell the story standing still, so I moved around, faced different parts of the audience at times, paced slowly when thoughtful and more quickly when agitated. Sometimes I stopped totally when struck by a particularly striking or troubling thought. Occasionally I turned to the imaginary traveling companion, and when the stranger drew near, I helped the people to "see" him. When the revelation at the table took place, I portrayed for them in gesture and facial expression the mingled confusion, delight, and consternation that flashed across the disciples' faces as they suddenly understood, only to have the stranger promptly disappear. Then were the hurried return to Jerusalem and the ecstatic welcome of the other disciples. How could anyone tell this story without being mobile?

flexibility

There is a strange sense in which preaching, which some people dismiss as the worst kind of opinionated monologue, is in fact a dialogue. Dr. Lloyd-Jones expressed it simply:

> The preacher while speaking should in a sense be deriving
> something from his congregation. There are those present in the

congregation who are spiritually minded people, and filled with the Spirit, and they make their contribution to the occasion. There is always an element of exchange in true preaching.[3]

Using much more dramatic language, John Broadus said this of a preacher:

> If, full of his theme and impressed with its importance, [he] presently secures the interested and sympathizing attention of even a few good listeners, and the fire of his eyes comes reflected back from theirs, till electric flashes pass to and fro between them, and his very soul glows and blazes and flames, he cannot fail sometimes to strike out thoughts more splendid and more precious than ever visit his mind in solitary musing.[4]

There is always an element of exchange in true preaching.

I must admit that I haven't exactly caught the reflecting of my fire in their eyes, and I'm not sure if that is the fault of my fire or their eyes, but I do know what both these esteemed gentlemen mean. Being free enough to move about and look into the eyes of the congregation gives the preacher a running commentary on how the message is getting across. It's amazing what a thoughtful nod can do for a preacher who is not sure if he's making things clear. But more importantly, if the preacher sees a look of total confusion or notices dozens of people turning to their spouses and mouthing, "What did he say?" he knows that an adjustment or clarification is necessary at once, if not sooner.

In the old Scottish kirks, there used to be a gentleman called the beadle. He carried a long pole with which to collect the tithes and

If people know there's a chance that the preacher will appear at the end of their pew during the sermon, they're much less likely to try to get in forty winks.

—◦◦◦—

offerings from the Scots and also, when necessary, to poke them during the sermon if they succumbed to slumber. No such preaching aids are available to the modern preacher, and if they were, they would probably be declared unconstitutional, so the preacher must use other methods to rescue people from slumber. The prerequisite of doing this is to be aware that they have departed, and this only the alert and flexible preacher will recognize. On one occasion when I was speaking, I noticed that a fair number of people were clearly having problems concentrating. One little child in the balcony expressed what the adults were feeling by giving vent to a massive, reverberating sigh. I promptly turned in the direction from which the heartfelt sigh originated and said, "I know exactly how you feel, honey. I was getting bored with this part, too, and so was everybody else. So I'll leave it and go on to the next part, and I'll get you out of here as quickly as I can." This, incidentally, marshaled the troops, and we lived to soldier on for a few more minutes.

proximity

Once, in a coffee bar outreach, I got into a conversation with a young man who said I was the first preacher he had been prepared to listen to. When I asked him why, he replied, "Because all preachers stand way up in their pulpits six feet above contradiction, but you come down on our level." Granted, the architecture of the average coffee bar differs drastically from a church, but I recognized that his point was valid. While for practical reasons, it is often necessary for a preacher to be raised above the congregation, it is all too easy for an invisible barrier to become erected between preacher and congregation. A sense of distance develops. No doubt some preachers like this, but modern people don't. Where distance has developed, communication suffers. But what can be done about it, particularly in a large auditorium?

A friend of mine used to ignore the beautiful carved pulpit in his traditional church and preach from the chancel steps. During his sermon he would occasionally move into the nave and address the people where they were sitting in their pews. This kind of mobility produced a great sense of rapport with the people and added greatly to their attention and involvement in the sermon. Let's face it: If people know there's a chance that the preacher will appear at the end of their pew during the sermon, they're much less likely to try to get in forty winks.

vitality

Dr. Donald Coggan, the former archbishop of Canterbury, wrote in his book *Stewards of Grace:* "It has been said that some men's sermons correspond to the psalmist's description of the activity of the Almighty on a chilly day, 'He casteth forth His ice like morsels: who is able to abide His frost?' "[5] This stinging comment reminds me of a remark one of my colleagues made to me when we worked together in a bank. He said, "Most churches are like bankers' dinners: cold and correct, decorous and dead."

―――――― ⌒⌒⌒ ――――――

"Most churches are like bankers' dinners:

cold and correct, decorous and dead."

―――――― ⌒⌒⌒ ――――――

Dr. Lloyd-Jones recounts the story of hearing a preacher speak on Jeremiah's testimony that the Word of God was like a fire in his bones. He said:

I left the service feeling that I had witnessed something quite extraordinary, for the one big thing that was missing in that service was "fire." The good man was talking about fire as if he were sitting on an iceberg…There was no zeal, no enthusiasm, no apparent concern for us as members of the congregation. His whole attitude seemed to be detached and academic and formal.[6]

Of course, personalities differ, and some preachers are more free and outgoing than others. As we have seen, preaching is the communication of truth through personality. So it is reasonable to assume that God will take his Word home to people's hearts through all kinds of personalities. But—and it is a big *but*—whatever the personality type of the preacher, there is no excuse for a lack of zeal and enthusiasm. The message of the gospel is, as Paul said, "the power of God for the salvation of everyone who believes" (Romans 1:16). We're talking power when we preach. We're talking salvation when we open our mouths. There's something potentially for everyone sitting out there as we stand before them. These are exciting and thrilling themes of monumental importance. They must send a quiver of excitement through the preacher who has been gripped by them, and they will put a sparkle in the eye that has pored over them. The heart gripped by the message beats faster, the voice by which the message is proclaimed betrays intensity of emotion and feeling. The body moves vigorously with the powerful inner energies of digested truth.

Some professors of preaching encourage their students to practice their gestures, voice pitch, volume, modulation, and tone before they

―――――――――― ⤳⤳⤳ ――――――――――

Never, ever neglect the inner filling of the Spirit and his gracious anointing as you embark on the ministry of preaching.

Preach It!

preach. I have no experience of this approach, but I worry that the preaching might come across as a well-rehearsed performance. Obviously the fact that the student is alerted to the need to give attention to these aspects of preaching is significant, and the result is much to be preferred to a flat, monotonous, stiff, and stilted presentation. But I suspect that once preachers have a little practice under their belts, have become comfortable enough in the preaching role to be natural, and have become intrigued and (dare I say it?) possessed by the message, the message will come forth with life and power—so much so that people may be able to say with more accuracy than usual, "Oh! I *see* what you are *saying!*"

Whatever the personality type of the preacher, there is no excuse for a lack of zeal and enthusiasm.

When all is said and done (and far more is usually said than done), there can never be such a thing as freshness in the preacher, the pulpit, and the pew independent of the refreshing work of the Spirit of God. All the technique in the world is no substitute, all the rhetorical skills known to man cannot take its place. Learn the techniques by all means, sharpen the God-given skills on every whetstone available, but never, ever neglect the inner filling of the Spirit and his gracious anointing as you embark on the ministry of preaching. Dr. J.I. Packer wrote in *The Gospel in the Modern World:*

> It is vital that the preacher should be full of the Holy Spirit for his task, so that he is clearheaded, warmhearted, ardent, earnest, and inwardly free to concentrate on the task of instruction and persuasion that each message imposes. An anointing

of the Spirit, therefore…is to be sought every time we preach. Beethoven wrote on the score of his Mass in D *(Missa Solemnis):* "From the heart it comes, to the heart may it go," and these same words should express the preacher's desire and prayer every time he ventures to speak.[7]

Endnotes

1. D. Martyn Lloyd-Jones, *Preaching and Preachers* (London: Hodder and Stoughton, 1971), 82.

2. Charles H. Spurgeon, *Lectures to My Students* (London: Marshall Pickering, first published 1954, reissued 1989), 276-77.

3. Lloyd-Jones, *Preaching and Preachers,* 84.

4. John A. Broadus, *On the Preparation and Delivery of Sermons* (New York: Harper and Row, 1870, new and revised edition 1944), 327.

5. Donald Coggan, *Stewards of Grace* (London: Hodder and Stoughton, 1958), 39.

6. Lloyd-Jones, *Preaching and Preachers,* 88.

7. Martyn Eden and David F Wells, ed., *The Gospel in the Modern World* (Downers Grove, Ill.: InterVarsity Press, 1991), 210-211.

——————————————— ⟞⟨o∕o∕o⟩⟝ ———————————————

"From the heart it comes,

to the heart may it go."

——————————————— ⟞⟨o∕o∕o⟩⟝ ———————————————

additional reading

Alexander, Eric J. *Plainly Teaching God's Word*. Toronto, Spiritual Life Conference.

Baxter, Richard. *The Reformed Pastor*. Edinburgh: The Banner of Truth Trust, first published 1656, reprinted 1989.

Bellah, Robert N. *Habits of the Heart*. New York: Harper and Row, 1986.

Berkley, James D., ed. *Leadership Handbooks of Practical Theology; Vol. 1, Word and Worship*. Grand Rapids, Mich.: Baker Books, 1992.

Bodey, Richard Allen, ed. *Inside the Sermon*. Grand Rapids, Mich.: Baker Books, 1990.

Briscoe, D. Stuart. *Expository Nuggets for Today's Christians*. Grand Rapids, Mich.: Baker Books, 1994.

_____. *Expository Nuggets From the Gospels*. Grand Rapids, Mich.: Baker Books, 1994.

Broadus, John A. *On the Preparation and Delivery of Sermons*. New York: Harper and Row, 1870, new and revised edition 1944.

Brooks, Phillips. *The Joy of Preaching*. Grand Rapids, Mich.: Kregel Publications, 1989.

Bryson, Harold T. *Expository Preaching*. Nashville, Tenn.: Broadman and Holman, 1995.

Buttrick, David. *Homiletic*. Philadelphia: Fortress Press, 1987.

Chapell, Bryan. *Christ-Centered Preaching*. Grand Rapids, Mich.: Baker Books, 1994.

Claypool, John R. *The Preaching Event.* San Francisco: Harper San Francisco, 1990.

Coggan, Donald. *Stewards of Grace.* London: Hodder and Stoughton, 1958.

Colquhohn, Frank. *Christian Foundations; Vol. 2, Christ's Ambassadors.* Philadelphia: Westminster Press, 1965.

Dallimore, Arnold. *Spurgeon.* Chicago: Moody Press, 1984.

Diduit, Michael, ed. *Handbook of Contemporary Preaching.* Nashville, Tenn.: Broadman Press, 1992.

Eden, Martyn, and David F. Wells, ed. *The Gospel in the Modern World.* Downers Grove, Ill.: InterVarsity Press, 1991.

Feathers, C.H. for Arrows Spurgeon. *The Quotable Spurgeon.* Wheaton, Ill.: Harold Shaw Publishers, 1990.

Fisher, Wallace E. *Who Dares to Preach?* Minneapolis: Augsburg, 1979.

Freeman, Harold. *Variety in Biblical Preaching.* Waco, Tex.: Word Books, 1987.

Hendricks, Howard G. *Teaching to Change Lives.* Portland, Oreg.: Multnomah Press, 1987.

Howard, J. Grant. *Creativity in Preaching.* Grand Rapids, Mich.: Zondervan, 1987.

Hybels, Bill, Stuart Briscoe, and Haddon Robinson. *Mastering Contemporary Preaching.* Portland, Oreg.: Multnomah Press, 1989.

Jowett, J.H. *The Preacher, His Life and Work.* Grand Rapids, Mich.: Baker Books, 1977.

Kinlaw, Dennis F. *Preaching in the Spirit.* Grand Rapids, Mich.: Francis Asbury Press of Zondervan Publishing House, 1985.

Lewis, Ralph L., and Gregg Lewis. *Inductive Preaching.* Westchester, Ill.: Crossway Books, 1983.

Lloyd-Jones, D. Martyn. *Preaching and Preachers.* London: Hodder and Stoughton, 1971.

Logan, Samuel T., Jr., ed. *The Preacher and Preaching.* Phillipsburg, N.J.: Presbyterian and Reformed Publishing Company, 1986.

Loscalzo, Craig A. *Preaching Sermons That Connect.* Downers Grove, Ill.: InterVarsity Press, 1992.

MacPherson, Ian. *The Art of Illustrating Sermons.* New York: Abingdon Press, 1964.

MacPherson-Johnston, Graham. *Preaching to a Postmodern World.* Grand Rapids, Mich.: Baker Books, 2001.

Marlin, George J., ed. *The Quotable Chesterton.* San Francisco: Ignatius Press, 1986.

McKenna, David L. *Renewing Our Ministry.* Waco, Tex.: Word Books, 1986.

Olford, David L., ed. *A Passion for Preaching.* Nashville, Tenn.: Thomas Nelson Publishers, 1989.

Olford, Stephen F. *Committed to Christ and His Church.* Grand Rapids, Mich.: Baker Books, 1991.

Olford, Stephen F., and David L. Olford. *Anointed Expository Preaching.* Nashville, Tenn.: Broadman and Holman, 1998.

Perry, Lloyd M. *A Manual for Biblical Preaching.* Grand Rapids, Mich.: Baker Books, 1965.

Perry, Lloyd M., and Charles M. Sell. *Speaking to Life's Problems.* Chicago: Moody Press, 1983.

Piper, John. *The Supremacy of God in Preaching.* Grand Rapids, Mich.: Baker Books, 1990.

Pitt-Watson, Ian. *A Primer for Preachers.* Grand Rapids, Mich.: Baker Books, 1986.

Richard, Ramesh. *Scripture Sculpture.* Grand Rapids, Mich.: Baker Books, 1995.

Robinson, Haddon W. *Biblical Preaching.* Grand Rapids, Mich.: Baker Books, 1980.

Sangster, W.E. *The Craft of the Sermon.* London: Epworth Press, 1954.

Shelley, Marshall. ed. *Changing Lives Through Preaching and Worship.* Nashville, Tenn.: Ballantine Books, 1995.

Simeon, Charles. *Evangelical Preaching.* Portland, Oreg.: Multnomah Press, 1986.

Skinner, Craig. *The Teaching Ministry of the Pulpit.* Grand Rapids, Mich.: Baker Books, 1973.

Spurgeon, Charles H. *Lectures to My Students.* London: Marshall Pickering, first published 1954, reissued 1989.

Stott, John R.W. *Between Two Worlds.* Grand Rapids, Mich.: Wm. B. Eerdmans, 1982.

_____. *The Contemporary Christian.* Downers Grove, Ill.: InterVarsity Press, 1992.

_____. *The Preacher's Portrait.* Grand Rapids, Mich.: Wm. B. Eerdmans, 1961.

Tannen, Deborah. *You Just Don't Understand.* New York: Ballantine Books, 1990.

Temple, William. *Readings in St. John's Gospel.* London: MacMillan, 1947.

Watson, David. *I Believe In the Church.* London: Hodder and Stoughton, 1978.

Wiersbe, Warren W. *Preaching and Teaching With Imagination.* Grand Rapids, Mich.: Baker Books, 1996.